By the same Editor
LAUGHTER BEFORE WICKET
(Allen and Unwin, 1986)

Laughter Before Wicket
The Second Innings

A Select Team of
18 Humorous Cricketing Stories

Edited by
PETER HAINING

Illustrated by
JOHN JENSEN

SOUVENIR PRESS

ISBN 0 285 63007 5

Phototypset by Input Typesetting Ltd, London
Printed and bound in Great Britain by
Biddles Ltd., Guildford & King's Lynn

This book is for:

*The Members of the
Duke of Scrotum's
Touring XI*

Contents

Introduction

One of the great traditions of cricket is the 'Select XI': the group of players brought together to fulfil a fixture, or perhaps a series of games, during the season. The participants may be of varying abilities—in fact, they usually are of *widely* varying abilities—but the pleasure to be had playing in such company is one of the joys of the game. I know all about this because most of my cricketing experience has been with teams of writers or local village players.

The 'Select XI' tradition can be traced back through all the years that cricket has been played, and for almost as long in literature. Who, for example, is not familiar with Charles Dickens' account of the uproarious match between Dingley

9

Dell and All-Muggleton in *The Pickwick Papers*, which he wrote in 1836? Indeed, authors and journalists have been among those most devoted to the tradition. A century ago, to cite another example, J. M. Barrie, the author of *Peter Pan*, was regularly assembling his literary friends under the strange name of the Allahakbarries XI, and today the same spirit lives on in games like the annual fixture of *The Spectator* magazine v. The Coach and Horses, the Soho public house immortalised by Jeffrey Bernard.

All such games are, inevitably, prone to moments of humour, either unintentional or deliberate. Sometimes even the thought of the matches can bring a smile to the face: imagine, for instance, the sight of the eleven Greenwich pensioners with one *arm* who played an equal number of veterans from the same locality with one *leg* at the Oval in 1852! Or perhaps the slightly less curious but doubtless equally keenly fought meeting of National Hunt jockeys and professional boxers!

If you want to contemplate some unusual fixtures, how about the team from the Commonwealth War Graves Commission who in 1989 played the Venerable English College in Italy for the 'Rome Ashes'; or the 'Test Match' in July 1987 between the crews of the British nuclear submarine *Superb* and the American submarine *Sea Devil*, which was played at the North Pole in a temperature of fifteen degrees below freezing! According to a report I read, the stumps had to be set in aluminium holders to grip the ice, and pads and gloves were worn over survival kit. Although the ball apparently bounced exactly the same as it does on grass, there was a real problem with fielding, for when any fielder ran after the ball he found it impossible to stop. (As a matter of record, the British won by twelve runs and fewer chilblains!)

There have been some bizarre results in this type of *ad hoc* cricket, too. In another cold spot, Helsinki, in 1879, a team of expatriate Englishmen beat All Lappland after the Lapps were all out for nought in the second innings. More recently, in May 1986, in a game in Sussex, Keymer and Hassocks v. Ashdown, the home side achieved the respectable score of 182 for five and then proceeded to bowl out their visitors without a single run, no-ball, wide or even a bye being conceded!

One must not forget the ladies, either, for women have been playing the game for almost two hundred and fifty years, the first all-female encounter having taken place in June 1745 at Gosden Common, Bramley, Surrey, between 'XI Maids of Bramley' and 'XI Maids of Hambleton'. The girls played in the most fetching half-hooped skirts with (for decency's sake!) ankle-concealing pantaloons, and red or blue hair ribbons to denote which side they were on. It was the Hambleton ladies who went into the record books as the very first winners in women's cricket by just eight runs.

Women also play the game on the faraway Pacific island of New Caledonia. The sport was introduced by some Australian missionaries, but was quickly adapted to local requirements. The girls play in bare feet and dress in colourful sarongs, and have a bowler and wicket-keeper at *both* ends to speed up the game. There are no off-side fielders, to make for more excitement, not to mention runs. The role of the men on this Melanesian island, where cannibalism was practised until not so long ago, is traditionally limited to scoring!

Best of all, though, I like the story of the young Australian weekend cricketer who played in two games *simultaneously*. Ian Smith started one afternoon a few years back batting for Mansfield Hosiery Mills v. Bywater Clay Cross, but lost his wicket cheaply. On an adjoining pitch, another team was playing with a man short and—with the permission of the captain of the Mansfield side—borrowed Smith. He promptly scored a hundred and then returned to field for his original team! There was, I am sorry to report, an unhappy sequel to this unique achievement, for Ian and his captain were reported for the incident and both were banned for two games!

Such stories are food and drink not just for cricket club annual dinners, but for writers on the sport as well. And over the years I have noticed how a number of humorists—who also happen to be cricket lovers—have seized upon this tradition of laughter before wicket as the inspiration for some very funny articles and short stories.

Now, although I have never captained an XI of my own, the ambition is there—and this book probably represents the closest I'll ever get to that cherished dream. What I have done is pick a 'team' of eleven of my favourite humorists (plus a twelfth man and the inevitable small group of light-hearted pavilion commentators) and selected what I believe to be among their funniest cricketing stories. All of them, as you will read, played the game to some degree or other, which naturally adds piquancy to their contributions.

Indeed, I have to say that if I were asked to spend a hot summer's day on a village green while willow was brought to bear on leather, these are the men in whose company I'd ideally like to be. Of course the disparate ages from which they are drawn would require divine intervention to make the game possible, but in cricket surely *all* things are possible.

History is full of anecdotes illustrating the obsession many people have with cricket and the amusement this has provoked. It was John Arlott who not only first alerted me to the rich variety of humour to be found in cricket writings but also perfectly summarised this obsession. 'The fact is,' he said in those rich and resonant tones of his which delighted listeners for years, 'that cricket has divided the peoples of the world into two kinds—the fools who fall victim to its many delights and the fools who do not.'

I imagine, dear reader, as you have picked up this book, that you are one of the former. Welcome to the team!

Peter Haining
Boxford, Suffolk
May 1990

Village Cricket

by HARRY GRAHAM

There is probably nobody better suited to open a collection of stories such as this than Harry Graham, author of the classic Ruthless Rhymes, *and a real cricketing enthusiast. In fact I suspect that if Harry accepted my invitation to play, I'd turn the captaincy over to him because he was the captain of a Surrey village side for many years as well as being a reliable opening batsman.*

Harry's love of the game is in evidence in a number of his books, in particular in the stories of Reginald Drake Biffin, an almost Wodehousian figure who reputedly knows 'something about everything and everything about something'. Like his creator, Biffin is a cricket enthusiast, and there are several amusing tales about his exploits against the background of County and Test matches. But Harry's heart was somehow always closest to the village game, and a lifetime of experience of the vagaries and humours of such matches is distilled into this opening contribution. So, let play commence!

Correct dress

1

IT would, of course, be presumptuous to attempt at this period of the world's history to say anything original upon a subject so hackneyed as cricket. No Englishman requires instruction in a pastime with which he is familiar from his birth, nor is there any necessity to recommend so deservedly popular a pursuit. For, although there has of late been much idle criticism of the game, and many foolish suggestions have been made for enlivening it from a spectacular point of view, there seems little likelihood of its ever being ousted from the high place it still holds in the public favour.

To the ignorant and uninitiated cricket may doubtless occasionally appear a dull and dreary sport, just as in like fashion chess may seem tedious enough to the unintelligent onlooker, while the hectic delights of 'spilikins' are commonly hidden from the gaze of the casual observer. Even experts have at times been known to fall into a troubled sleep in the pavilion at Lord's on a hot summer's afternoon while watching the manoeuvres of a couple of conscientious batsmen who have taken an hour to compile twenty runs, and are evidently labouring under the delusion that they are engaged in an eight-day match. But although it may be true that first-class cricket does not appeal to every taste, there is one form of the game which no sane person can fail to enjoy. This particular branch of the sport in question can never justly be called tame (if a branch could ever be designated by so inappropriate an epithet), since it combines the peculiar charms of American baseball with the excitement of the Spanish bullfight and much of the anxious futility of patience. I refer, as I need hardly add, to what is technically known as Village Cricket.

Village Cricket! What blessed memories those two simple words recall to the minds of most of us! We seem to behold once more the village green of our happy youth, with the Jubilee Pump at one end competing ineffectually with the 'Bull and Kingfisher' at the other. We see the little church—recently restored by Messrs Burling and Glammer, who have picturesquely fitted the Norman Tower with a steeple and replaced the unhygienic stone font (in which William Rufus is said to have been baptised) by a more sanitary, modern contrivance of porcelain and pitch pine—overshadowing the tin 'Wesleyan Workmen's Club'; the post office, where acid drops and giant bull's-eyes are ever on sale; and the blacksmith's shop, with its glowing forge, where doubtless the anvil's music still thrills the youthful bosom. We smell the scent of wallflowers wafted from the Vicarage garden, mixing with the warm fragrance of new-mown lawn and the less agreeable perfume of the children as they stream from the school hard by. We note the athletic figure of the worthy curate, dragging the roller back and forth across that exiguous patch of comparatively smooth turf opposite the porch of the village inn where the rival teams have already gathered to refresh themselves for the coming contest.

See! Here comes the young Squire on his bicycle clad in immaculate flannels, and bearing the long green canvas bag whence he shall presently extract that supply of bats, pads, and other cricketing paraphernalia with which the village sportsman invariably omits to provide himself. Already the bails are being reverently laid upon the stumps by Mr Bunting, Lord Bumblefoot's butler from the Manor House, a stately, pontifical figure whose fitness for the post of umpire is as unquestioned as that of his colleague Mr Turmats, head gardener at the Vicarage, who is fulfilling a similar office at the other end of the pitch.

The Reverend Alfred Pertwee, than whom no more robust Christian ever intoned the Athanasian Creed, is busy arranging the 'fields'. Jasper Marling, the blacksmith, moistens the ball in the most natural manner possible, preparatory to delivering a series of those deadly 'daisy-cutters' which have made his bowling famous throughout the countryside, from Chipping Winston to Goudbury—aye, and as far afield as Rollington and Murk End! The two sturdy batsmen who are to open the match for the Minshurst eleven advance from the little white scorer's tent, where the landlord of the 'Bull and Kingfisher' sits with moist pencil poised to record the first incident of the day's play. In another moment Mr Bunting will give the signal, Jasper Marling will grasp the ball in his gnarled fingers, and the great match will commence.

2

This is neither the time nor the place to describe in detail a game of village cricket. But for the benefit of any of my readers whose experience thereof may be limited, who may, however, at any moment be called upon to engage in this delightful sport, I propose to give one or two hints that I myself have found infinitely useful on such occasions as I have been tempted or coerced into taking part, whether in the character of captain, umpire, batsman, bowler or fieldsman (commonly called 'field').

The captain's position is one, as I need hardly say, of extreme responsibility. To be successful he needs common sense and tact, he must be a diplomat as well as a born leader of men. It is for him to arrange the order in which various members of his team shall bat, and he will invariably find that the individual distaste for going in first is only surpassed in intensity by the universal objection to going in last. In such circumstances he will require unusual powers of persuasion to solve a complicated and often painful problem.

When his team takes the field, the choice of bowlers rests with him, and it is he who must dispose the 'fields' in the positions best suited to their peculiar talents. Should Jasper Marling bowl eight consecutive 'no-balls', should four of the left-handed 'lobs' of 'Erbert Perks (the stableman from the Hall) be hit over the Wesleyan Workmen's Club, while the last ball of the 'over' goes skimming through the roof of the Vicar's greenhouse, it is for the captain to hint as delicately as possible that a change of bowling would be advisable. When Bill Turmats (the umpire's son), who is standing in a trance at 'long-leg' among the tall nettles that surround the Jubilee Pump, has on three separate occasions shown a marked disinclination to allow a skied catch to impinge upon his tender palms, it is for the captain to suggest that his position in the deep field might be more suitably occupied by the young Squire, and that Master Turmats should take the latter's place at 'point', where, if a ball comes at all, it will probably not give him time to get out of its way.

The captain should, in fact, be a man of strong personality, who can control his team in such a manner as to avoid any undue friction arising from jealousy or disappointed hopes. He must, in a word, inspire perfect confidence, and for this purpose nothing is more valuable than the ability to win the toss for innings. That this feat can be achieved without fraud or trickery I am assured by a very keen devotee of village cricket, a well-known writer, of unblemished reputation, deeply honoured and respected by all who know him, who has kindly explained to me the secret which I now propose to pass on to my readers.

Let us assume that the rival teams are mustered in the bar

parlour of the 'Bull and Kingfisher' before the game begins. While the pint pots are being replenished for the tenth time the captain of the visitors comes up to you and suggests in a friendly fashion that you and he should toss for the choice of innings.

'By all means,' you heartily reply, fumbling in your pocket just long enough to allow your antagonist time to produce a coin from his own.

'*You* cry,' he generously exclaims, as he spins his shilling into the air, where it gyrates for a few seconds before finally falling to the ground.

This is your opportunity. Before the shilling has come to rest you must shout, 'The Bird!' in a loud, clear voice. Having done so, walk across to the spot where the coin is now lying, and, after a brief inspection of its exposed surface, add: 'Hooray! we've won the toss!' You can then turn to your rival with a word or two of sympathy, as you break the news to him that you intend your team to bat first.

It does not in the least matter whether the shilling falls on its head or on its tail. If you have cried 'The Bird!' with sufficient vigour and self-confidence, the visiting captain will politely assume that this is a local term for whichever side of the coin is uppermost, as, indeed, you may perhaps deceive yourself into fancying that it is. Your decision will consequently be accepted without argument, all parties will be satisfied, and you can stroll across to the tent and put on your pads with a comparatively easy conscience. I may add that I myself have practised this method for the last two seasons and have never known it fail. Indeed, it is to a large extent due to my skill in winning the toss that this year I have again been elected captain of the Little Wilmingdon Wanderers, a post that I am otherwise wholly unqualified to fill.

3

Next to the captain it may truly be asserted that the unpire occupies the most important position in the village cricket field. It is not enough that he should be thoroughly acquainted with the laws of the game, be a man of wide experience and alert eye, prompt to decide knotty points, of unquestioned integrity, and, if possible, unrelated by marriage to any of the players. Besides all this he must be well versed in those questions of subtle etiquette, those chivalrous niceties of conduct, the practice of which may be said to distinguish village cricket from the more serious game played upon county grounds. If, for instance, the Earl of Bumblefoot condescends to take part in a local match, and before he has made (let us say) half a dozen runs is unluckily caught at the wicket, it is the duty of the umpire to say 'Not out!' in a clear voice just as his lordship starts to walk away towards the pavilion. In like fashion he should continue to say 'Not out!' to any appeals that may be made until Lord Bumblefoot has compiled some five-and-twenty runs. Then, and not before, is it permissible to give the Lord of the Manor 'out', if it is quite plain that the elderly nobleman has enjoyed as long an innings as he desires and would welcome an opportunity for repose. Again, if young Viscount Memlingham, Lord Bumblefoot's half-witted heir, elects to bowl for an over or two, the discreet umpire will close his eyes to any 'wides', or 'no-balls', and, should the bowler deliver a well-directed full-pitch that strikes the batsman on the head, and appeal for 'leg before wicket', he will say, 'Out, my lord!' without a moment's hesitation.

Among an umpire's most responsible duties are, first of all, the duty of giving a batsman 'guard' (or 'block' as it is sometimes entitled), and secondly the duty of calling 'Over!' when five (or in some cases six) fair balls have been delivered by any one bowler. The task of taking 'guard' requires no special aptitude. As soon as the batsman holds his bat in front of the wicket and clears his throat loudly enough to attract the unpire's attention, the latter should respond by gazing earnestly down the pitch, holding his right hand in the air and waggling it gently from right to left. In answer to these signals the batsman will at once move his bat in the direction indicated. The umpire should then waggle his hand from left to right, and when the batsman has replaced his bat in its original position he can remark, 'Two leg!' return to his place beside the wicket, and allow the bowler to commence his deadly work.

The duty of counting the balls in any 'over' is not always so easy as it sounds. The umpire's thoughts may wander, or his attention may be temporarily diverted by extraneous incidents such as the straying of a cow upon the pitch, the sight of his offspring tumbling down the Jubilee Well, or the still more harrowing spectacle supplied by those members of the batting team whose innings are happily over and who are tracing their eager footsteps towards the 'Bull and King-fisher'. Again, when a bowler has delivered four 'no-balls' and a couple of 'wides', when his three next balls have been hit out of bounds and twenty minutes have been spent searching for them among the Vicar's calceolaria, and when the tenth ball accidentally takes a wicket, it requires uncommon mathematical gifts to enable an umpire to remember how many more balls the bowler is justified in delivering.

In order to facilitate this arduous task some umpires provide themselves with five (or six) pennies, which they place in a convenient pocket, and then, as each ball is delivered, transfer one of these coins to another pocket, until the supply is exhausted and they may conclude by a system of logical computation that it is time to shout 'Over!' I remember, however, doing this once with rather disastrous results in 1885 at Tonbridge, where a Pan-Anglican Synod was being held, and a cricket match—'High Church v. Low Church'—had been arranged between two clerical teams on the county ground. (It may here be said that in other respects the game proved an immense attraction, and the gate-money, which was devoted to a fund for the conversion of infidels and heretics, is said to have achieved wonderful results in Asia Minor, where the two Turkish converts were so benighted that they had never realised that they were infidels or heretics until assured of this fact by the worthy Anglican prelate, whose mission it was to enlighten them.) On the occasion of this match I unfortunately forgot that the pocket in which I secreted my little umpire's hoard of coins was already occupied by a certain number of loose pennies which I habitually kept there for the purpose of tipping taxi-drivers. It was not until a High Church bowler had sent down eighteen consecutive balls and the crowd began to 'barrack' us that I realised that my supply of copper coinage would outlive the patience of the public, and hastily shouted 'Over!' just as the indignant populace began to set fire to the pavilion.

4

The conduct of the batsman upon a humble village cricket ground differs in but the smallest particulars from that of his brother batsman at Lord's or the Oval. Unless, however, he wishes to acquire a reputation for pride and vain-gloriousness, which he will find it difficult to live up to, he should be very careful never to appear at the wicket attired in more than *one* pad. If he conscientiously finds it necessary to protect his fingers from a fast bowler he may also wear *one* glove, but it must be a *left-hand* glove and should be worn on the *right* hand.

The downfall of the batsman's wicket whom he is destined to follow is the signal for him to hurry out of the refreshment tent, where he has been artificially stimulating his courage, and help his predecessor to doff his pad. This he should transfer to his own left leg with as little loss of time as possible, buckling it as he walks to the wicket—always a difficult task—or perhaps soliciting the assistance of the umpire. As soon as he has been given 'guard' (as explained above) he must proceed to excavate a trench about six inches deep, a foot in rear of the popping-crease, and when these digging operations are completed he should walk slowly up the pitch, carefully levelling any uneven portions of the ground, rooting out plantains, removing stones, and patting the sward with his bat wherever he deems such treatment necessary. Then, glancing round to see where the various 'fields' are stationed, he should moisten the palms of his hands, twirl his bat two or three times round his head, and face the bowler with such confidence as he may possess.

Half the success of making a big score at village cricket lies in the batsman's ability to establish a 'funk' in the ranks of his opponents. This may sometimes be done by advancing up the pitch with one's bat raised in a threatening attitude as soon as the bowler begins that little run which is to terminate with the delivery of a ball. From sheer terror the bowler will probably send down a loose full-pitch to leg which can be hit into the cemetery for six, and when this process has been repeated several times his nerves will be completely shattered and there is no reason why the batsman should ever get out. Of course, if the bowler keeps his wits about him he has merely to lob the ball over the batsman's head and the wicket-keeper will stump the latter before he can return to his crease; this, however, is a risk that must be faced.

Custom lays down certain minor by-laws governing the conduct to be adopted by a batsman whose innings is at an end and who wishes to return to the pavilion or tent with ease and dignity. Should he have scored, say, a dozen runs he may walk calmly away from the wicket, unbuttoning his glove as he goes. If his score has reached twenty, his return to the tent will be greeted with wild applause, when he should break into a slow trot as he approaches the spectators, touching his hat every few yards in acknowledgement of their cheers. Should he have compiled fifty runs he may start running directly he leaves the wicket and sprint briskly and with bared head to the shelter of the tent. If, however, he has made what is technically known as a 'duck's egg', he should avoid all expressions of annoyance, should never throw his bat away with an oath or attempt to break it across his knee, but he may pardonably creep on all fours from the wicket to the back entrance of the 'Bull and Kingfisher', and there drown his woes in the only satisfactory fashion possible.

5

There are certain minor rules of etiquette to which the village bowler should conform if he wishes to command the respect of his peers. It is usual, for instance, when the captain of your side asks you to try a few 'overs' at the church end, to express surprise at his choice of a bowler, to say that you haven't had a ball in your hand since you left school (which is, of course, a lie), and that you're afraid your arm will be very stiff. You should then remove your hat and hang it on the umpire, take off your 'sweater' and drape it round that worthy's shoulders, give him your watch and chain, your silver cigarette case, your pipe and (after counting it carefully) any loose change you may have in your pockets. If, however, you feel compelled to remove your boots—as may sometimes be necessary if the wicket is wet and slippery— you should on no account hang these on the umpire, but rather place them neatly together behind the stumps, where they will be in nobody's way. You may then try a preliminary ball or two at the side of the pitch, though it invariably happens that the wicket-keeper fails to stop these trial balls and a certain amount of delay ensues while they are being retrieved from the Jubilee Pump. When you feel that your arm is sufficiently loose, measure out the run that you intend to take behind the wicket, mark the starting-point by digging your heel into the turf or erecting a cairn of daisies, and take good care to attract the batsman's attention before you deliver your first ball.

The bowler who can fill his antagonists with panic is clearly half-way on the road to success. This can sometimes be done by assuming a ferociously professional air, and with this in view it is always a good plan to alter the position of as many of the fieldsmen as possible before you start to bowl. Beckon to 'cover-point' to come closer in, ask 'third man' to draw a bit wider, signal to 'long-leg' to go deeper—move the fields about, in fact, in any way you like so long as by so doing you create in the batsman's mind the impression that you really do know something about the technical side of the game. If, too, you can so arrange matters that your first ball should strike him in a vital part he will be more than ever inclined to treat any subsequent balls with redoubled respect.

Personally, I have often found that by taking a very long run of about a hundred yards, dodging behind the umpire at the last moment, and bowling the ball from the side of the wicket where the batsman least expected to see me, I have often succeeded where other more skilful bowlers failed. Peculiar forms of action are also at times efficacious. I used at one time to be able to make the batsman think that I was about to deliver a slow left-handed 'googly', and then suddenly sling in a swift right-handed 'grub' while the wretched man's eye was still riveted upon my waving left arm. Again, I would sometimes follow a slow ball right up the pitch and dance about in front of the batsman as though with the intention of catching him out off the end of his bat; this, however, required considerable courage, and I gave it up in 1907, when an unaffrighted player drove the ball back at my head with such violence as to knock out six of my teeth, and then proceeded to run eight runs while I was still searching for missing molars among the plantains.

6

For the fieldsman there is no particular code of manners. The great thing for him to remember is that the ball should be fielded and returned to the wicket as quickly as possible. In order to save a boundary hit it is quite allowable to jump on the ball, but the practice of throwing one's hat at it in a vain attempt to arrest its flight has fallen into abeyance (if not desuetude).

Experience alone can teach a man who is stationed in the deep field how to run towards a high catch in such a fashion that although he will seem to be covering the ground very rapidly there is really no danger of his reaching the ball before it touches the ground. Should he miscalculate the distance and find it impossible, with decency, to prevent the ball falling into his hands (whence, of course, it will rebound upon the sward), he should point apologetically at the sun (which is probably behind his back) or pretend to nurse a wounded finger. It is as well to remember, too, that whenever a ball hits a batsman's pad, it is correct for *every* member of the fielding team to shout 'How's that?' in as confident a tone as possible, and thus perhaps by sheer force of sound intimidate the umpire into saying 'Out!'

Some people, I admit, consider this a practice that should be viewed with disfavour—that it should, in fact, be placed in that category of reprehensible acts which are so entirely out of place in village cricket that it will be only necessary to mention one or two of them here. When, for example, a ball strikes one's bat and bounds into the wicket-keeper's hands, it is not considered good form to rub one's elbow as though suffering acute pain, nor will such action deceive anybody. Again, nothing is so criminal as for a wicket-keeper to pretend to throw the ball back to the bowler, and then, when the batsman, assuming that he is immune from attack, walks out into the pitch to inspect a worm-cast, to seize the opportunity of stumping him. Last of all, let me say that the bowler who draws a batsman's notice to an imaginary aeroplane in the sky, and then slings down a fast 'yorker' that takes his wicket, is only one degree less base than the deep field who pretends he has lost the ball in the long grass and then, when the umpire and both batsmen come to help him to find it, picks it suddenly from his pocket and tries to throw down the untenanted wicket. These things, I need hardly say, are not done on any of those

village cricket grounds where Englishmen consort together
to engage in the best of all games, and incidentally to acquire
those sterling qualities that help to make England what she
is.

   Much of our national greatness, believe me, depends upon
the lessons our fellow-countrymen have learnt from time
immemorial upon many an obscure village green. Never
was truer word spoken than by the Iron Duke when he said
that the Battle of Waterloo was won upon the playing-fields
at Eton; the memory of this immortal epigram still sends a
thrill through the breast of every true Englishman, unless,
of course, he happens to have been privately educated in a
clergyman's family at Wigan. Patience, chivalry, persever-
ance, all our national virtues are to a great extent the fruit
of early training on the cricket ground. To it we owe the
dogged determination, the fearless courage, which express
themselves today in that square, resolute jaw that Britons
have inherited from a long succession of cricketing ancestors;
indeed, we may justly affirm that it is largely due to village
cricket that, as the Psalmist so felicitously puts it, the chins
of the fathers are visited upon the children, unto the third
and fourth generation.

How Our Village Tried to Play the Australians

by HUGH DE SELINCOURT

The second man in my team has to be the all-rounder Hugh de Selincourt who, in his tales of village cricket at Tillingfold, begun in the 1930s, anticipated the current series by Peter Tinniswood about Whitney Scrotum. In fact, it was difficult for me to decide whether to include one of Peter's hilarious 'Tales from a Long Room', recounted by the irascible Brigadier, or a contribution from Hugh's bag of Tillingfold delights. I opted for Hugh in the end because he was also an opening bowler, could score freely from well up the order and played regularly for an Authors' XI.

Tillingfold, which 'lies in a hollow under the Downs', is the archetypal English village, and stories of the many doughty battles fought on its field of play are to be found in his books such as Over!, Move Over! and The Cricket Match—the last of which J. M. Barrie called 'the best book ever written about cricket'. Hugh believed passionately that village cricket was the purest of all English games, a view he expressed in a much-reprinted essay, 'Ours is the Real Cricket'.

As its title indicates, the story which follows should perhaps be subtitled 'A Cricketing Fantasy', for what it relates is probably the dream of any stalwart who believes that he and his team could do what England sides have so palpably failed to achieve in most recent Test series. It is a wholly entertaining tale in Hugh's skilful hands, and I would certainly recommend those readers who are here getting their first taste of his writing to seek out others of his books, for he and Peter Tinniswood are the masters of this form of storytelling.

27

No one knows or will ever know now how the secret leaked out, and turned what was to be essentially an informal and friendly affair into an event of national, nay, world-wide importance. It was natural enough that the present Australian team should wish to have a go at the village which had been audacious enough even to dream of beating Mr Armstrong's victorious eleven; and the match had been arranged on the understanding that they would turn up in time to start at 2.30 exactly like any other team: tea 5, draw 6.45 or 7.15 if there was anything in it: then a glass of beer perhaps at the pub and a nice drive home to their quarters in the cool of the summer evening. They had heard much of our pretty village grounds which are unknown in Australia, all grass being burnt up by the heat, and were anxious to have a game on one. 'Oh yes, pass the word round certainly in surrounding villages, boys; but keep it to yourselves, you understand, all private like and incog.'

The news appeared first as a rumour (the match was entered X on the Tillingfold card), then the rumour was described as a hoax, which was fiercely denied. The British

Broadcasting Corporation mentioned the matter in neat English with a courteous smile, and the world pricked up its ears. The thing suddenly became a gigantic stunt. The national game played in its natural surroundings: the village green is the home of cricket: a noble gesture illustrative of all that is finest in democracy: the snobbery of Test Matches: the fatal respect of persons degraded the freedom which was the birthright of every Briton . . . There was no slogan, political or social or religious, that was not tacked somehow on to this little game. And astute financiers saw there was money in it: the suggestion was actually made that the game should be played by artificial light at Olympia. But the climax was reached when Mr Hitler, who dictates to a neighbouring country, decided that here was the golden opportunity for his Nazis to learn about the great English game in its simplest yet grandest form: the running commentary translated into German was to be broadcast throughout the length and breadth of his Reich, to battalions of Nazis drawn up in ranks to listen. Pictures of the game, with elucidatory comment, were to be thrown on every screen: an intensive course of cricket culture (to be known always under drastic penalties as Hitler-ball) was arranged to start from this one game, which as I have said was intended to be a friendly and informal affair. The Soviet, French and Italian governments, growing suspicious, sent secret agents to investigate. Many serious persons wrote to serious papers urging the necessity of an international conference at Geneva to discuss all possible implications, before an encounter which might have such far-reaching consequences on world welfare should take place.

The effect of all this publicity upon the village team was both distressing and unpleasant. Tillingfold have, for one reason and another, experienced some difficulty in raising a side at all this season. This world-hubbub made it clear, as the great day drew nearer, that the difficulty of raising a side for this important match would be well-nigh insuperable. Natural diffidence caused our fellows to shrink from makin' monkeys of themselves, as one man put it: another man declined to be treated like a bloody film star and be paid nothing for his pains.

In consequence it became increasingly difficult to raise a side, but Mr Gauvinier, faced with the ignominy of turning out one or even two men short when the eyes of the Empire were upon him, and of asking Mr Woodfull to oblige with a couple of substitutes when the ears of the world were pricked to catch his voice, eventually succeeded in getting a fairly representative side together, even though he was seriously upset by receiving an urgent message marked Strictly Confidential from Headquarters, giving him a hint, large as the imprint of an elephant's foot and even weightier, as to the extreme inadvisability of employing in his attack upon the Australian batsmen anything even remotely resembling Leg Theory or anything that might possibly be construed into Leg Theory. In fact, under the circumstances, considering the unfortunate state of Japanese trade rivalry, it might be wiser perhaps to have no man at all, except a mid-on well back, upon the leg-side, when the more important batsmen were at the wicket.

Thus an avalanche of extraneous matter descended upon the game and bade fair to wreck and bury it, as the snow thundering down the mountain-side may wreck and bury an Alpine village.

On Wednesday morning the ground looked peaceful and smiling in the sunshine as it usually looks of a fine morning: a few toddlers staggered about on the pleasant stretch of mown grass, as they usually do, greatly daring but not too far from their prams and their mothers. The square on which the wickets were to be pitched waited expectant, full of promise, full of that happy promise, which only a cricket ground packed with stored memories of good games won and good games lost can ever give in all its richness of unforgettable incident. On Wednesday afternoon came the first sign of what was to happen. A motor-car with trailer attached drew up by the gate leading into the ground: its occupants got out, looked round, saw a farmhouse near, called at the farm, and were seen to return, slowly drive car and trailer into the adjoining field and come to a slow stop. First one by one they came, then in twos, then in threes, and settled in the adjoining fields, as gipsies come from all over England to settle on the course at Epsom. By Friday the thing began to look serious: and the British Broadcasting Corporation kindly consented to make a statement in their news items to the effect that the cricket match which was undoubtedly to be played between Tillingfold and the Australians was essentially a friendly and intimate affair; that listeners should be reminded that the accommodation on a village ground was strictly limited, unlike Old Trafford or Trent Bridge or the Oval, where thousands could watch the play in comparative comfort. And so on and so on. The announcement was, of course, beautifully worded and exquisitely spoken, but its effect, however well intentioned, was unfortunate: for the average listener thought 'Oh that's all right, then: nobody will be turning up, so there'll be plenty of room for us.' And forthwith determined to make a day of it.

From every town within reach, moreover (and what town now is not within reach?), charabanc and coach proprietors prepared excursion parties (with lunch and tea included in the fare) to see the match. On Friday night the stream of traffic began to flow; early on Saturday morning it was in full spate; from North and West and East, converging upon Tillingfold; a vast concourse of vehicles. By midday there were evidences of such a traffic block as had hitherto been unknown in the short history of motoring. The Authorities, with the help of the A.A. and the R.A.C., did what they could, but they were powerless: our village policeman was wonderful, but what could one man effect against this national obsession? Mr Gauvinier began to have serious fears that those of his team who went to work at any distance might be unable to reach their homes in time to have dinner and change: and that those who lived a mile or so outside the village would be unable to reach the ground at all. He was all right himself, as he could walk by field-paths most of the way; to bicycle, as was his usual practice, was quite out of the question. But what would others do? Just as he was leaving the house the telephone bell rang. He was thankful that he had not disconnected it, as rage and despair at its persistent ringing for the last twenty-four hours had prompted him to do; for it was Mr Woodfull speaking. He was speaking from Shoreham. He had arranged not without difficulty to start an hour before his scheduled time but they were properly stuck at Shoreham. Dreadful. Yes. Have you heard? No. What, the Soviet? Yes, Stalin's mad Hitler's got the jump of him: when he's decreed days ago all good Russians must take to cricket. Sure? Oh yes, Foreign Office rang me up at 10.25. Oh we'll make it. Sure thing. And are you there? There's to be an American broadcast. Short-length wave. Yes. Sort of return for Kansas Derby. We'll get; but may be a trifle late. Some game. Yes. So long.

Mr Gauvinier started on his walk to the ground, cursing the foolish circumstances which caused him, an oldish man, to start the afternoon with a one-and-a-half-mile's walk carrying a cricket bag. It seemed, too, a great shame that Italy, France and Spain should be left out, as they appeared to be. He'd had such a happy time in Florence, he was half French: he'd always wanted to visit Spain, the home of Don Quixote and Sancho Panza. But the sight of the country lane that he was obliged to cross and along which he usually bicycled quietly to the ground, scattered these altruistic broodings. It was, for as far as he could see, a solid jam of motor vehicles of every description, from baby cars to the most enormous coaches on which he had ever (having missed the last Motor Show) set his astonished eyes.

'You goin' to play in the match? Coo! Er! I'm comin' in tow!' Gauvinier pretended not to hear: but it was no good. The cry was taken up like magic or wireless loud-speakered, and soon a seething, struggling mob (squabbling too, for it was shouted in expostulation, 'How'll you ever find your way back to your seat and what'll you do then miles away from anywhere?') was swarming in his company along the shaded pathway, known as Lovers' Lane. He overheard: 'Some sort of souvenir, to show the kids,' and became aware how violent and infectious is mass emotion, for he began to feel, as he quickened his pace, that he had somehow ceased to be a person and become merely (trousers, shirt, coat, bag and bag's contents) a compendium of possible souvenirs, likely to be dispersed at any moment.

A label on his cricket bag did the mischief: 'It's Govineer, the village captain!' came an excited shout.

He broke into a run: they gave chase, yelling to him as tasty a morsel to his greedy pursuers as ever hare to hounds. Had he not, with great presence of mind, dropped his bag to leave them scrambling and struggling for its contents, it is doubtful what would have happened to him: probably what happens to a Russian traveller when overtaken by hungry wolves on the snow-clad steppes. As it was he reached the ground whole in body but ruffled in spirit, or rather he reached the next field but one adjoining the ground.

Tum demum, then and not till then (so slow is even a moderately intelligent mind to grasp a situation outside its previous experience), the full extent of the catastrophe, which publicity had wrought upon what should have been a rather specially good little game, broke upon his consciousness. He was in fact almost as nonplussed as the Higher Military Command by the events of the Great War. Like them he simply did not know what to do. He could only murmur to himself, as he threaded his difficult way through cars and campers and hundreds ever anxious to press somehow nearer to the field of play: 'All I know is this isn't cricket!' Bagless, bootless, batless, padless, capless, he eventually arrived at what had been the ground, and now resembled some weirdly arranged sort of car park: and he, the stickler for punctuality, heard the monastery clock chime three above the babel.

'Barely room for a tennis court,' he sadly thought. 'No room at all for Tim Wall's run—if he should get here.'

'This is an outrage, sir,' a furious voice accosted him. 'An absolute disgrace. Do you realise this is a great occasion? Are these the best arrangements you folk are capable of making? Have you no sense of responsibility, no glimmer of what is fitting?'

'Yes. Yes. But I've no cricket boots,' was all Gauvinier could say.

'Grossly selfish and personal! No thought for the good name of the country: no thought for her prestige in the eyes of other nations. You saunter on to the ground half an hour late. It's an infamy!'

'Yes. Yes. But I've no cricket boots,' Gauvinier sadly repeated.

'Something's got to be done about it: and pretty sharp, too!'

'Oh, I agree!' said Gauvinier. 'But I have never played without cricket boots before!'

High words might have arisen between the village captain and the enraged Broadcasting Official, had not, most fortunately, their attention been distracted by the manœuvres of an aeroplane flying uncommonly low.

'Gosh! It's an autogiro. Look, there are two of them.'

All looked up: and large numbers were bumped in the back as they gazed up by eager photographers rushing forward with their cameras. 'Not on the wicket, please,' the distraught Gauvinier supplicated at the top of his voice, still thinking only of his wretched little game. His pitiful cry was not heard: with dismay he watched first one, then the other, slowly and beautifully alight upon the wicket. The crowd surged nearer to see Mr Woodfull emerge with his cricket bag from the first: Mr Bradman from the second. The cameras clicked; millions next day read the caption: *This picture shows Mr Woodfull arriving on the Tillingfold ground: eager for his encounter with the village.*

Mr Gauvinier found himself shaking hands with Mr Woodfull, and murmuring foolishly:

'Awfully sporting of you to have turned up. All this,' he waved a rueful hand, 'I'm most dreadfully sorry about it. Such a pretty little ground: never very large: now it is rather close quarters, I'm afraid.'

And Mr Woodfull, as behoves a visiting captain, remained dauntlessly courteous and cheerful, and assured him that he was certain they'd have a really jolly little game in spite of everything. Gauvinier shook a doubtful head.

'There's room perhaps to toss,' he said, extracting a half-crown from his trouser pocket. But even so simple and so pleasant a matter of routine as the toss was not permitted to take place without interference. On the instant two or three excited photographers leaped forward crying out: 'Just one moment, *please!*' in the harsh tone of authority curbing exasperation with incompetence. 'It's more usual for captains to toss in front of the pavilion in their cricket kits.'

'There is no front to the pavilion now: and I have no kit now . . .' Gauvinier mourned.

We may waive that. Now, left hand lightly placed in left trouser-pocket. So. Half-crown placed on right thumb-nail. So. Thank you. Your head turned slightly more this way. Mr Woodfull, please if you would step two paces nearer. Thank you. Three-quarter face to the camera.' 'Perhaps both gentlemen would not mind removin' their Trilbies,' suggested another photographer. 'What about Mr Bradman comin' into the picture?' a third suggested, which enraged a fourth who had been arranging to make a special and exclusive snap *Don Bradman watching the skipper toss.*

'Take us or leave us!' said Mr Woodfull, unused to being thus hectored, bluntly to the photographers, and added kindly to Mr Gauvinier: 'You just toss, old man.'

But Mr Woodfull's attention was distracted at that moment by the return of the autogiros. The welfare of his men was near to his heart, as it should be to the heart of every sound captain.

'Pack up, you fellows,' he shouted unceremoniously. 'Out of the way. Make a larger space, there. They must have room to alight.'

And he started to signal frantically to the 'planes, waving his hat in one hand and his handkerchief in the other.

Meanwhile Mr Bradman had slipped off, like the boy he is, merrily shouldering his way through the crowd, in search of coconut shies which he felt must be lurking in such precincts and for which he has a very great liking. He is accustomed to visit the fairs round Melbourne and Sydney in a small Ford van in which to take home his winnings, or if he should go with Mr Kippax or Mr McCabe, in a Leyland lorry. The proprietors of these and kindred forms of amusement were not the least thankful among Australian sportsmen when no untoward circumstance prevented the great Test team of 1934 from sailing for the shores of England.

Now, too, Mr Gauvinier's arm was gripped by the same Broadcasting Official, by this time almost completely distraught.

'Something's got to be done about it,' he babbled. 'Something's got to be done about it. We can't go on describing the rural scene for ever. Nobody could.'

'I tried to toss,' Gauvinier excused himself.

'Such shocking management is a disgrace to the country. Do you mean to tell me an English crowd is so unsporting as to ruin the very thing they have come miles and at great personal inconvenience to see?'

'I've told you nothing,' Gauvinier said. 'You can see for yourself it looks uncommonly like it. No one man by himself would do it: a mass of men together does.'

However, by 4.30 the last of the village team had fought his painful way on to what was left of the ground, dishevelled certainly, but determined (fair play being fair play) not to be crowded out of his well-earned Saturday's game by any mob of gaping sightseers. This proper bulldog spirit took them to the ground and then deserted them. They stood about miserably, powerless to help Gauvinier clear a slightly

larger space around the poor pitch. But Mr Gauvinier, elated
at having been at last allowed to toss and at having won it,
raised his voice and appealed to the better nature of the
crowd: and what man has ever made such an appeal to an
English crowd in vain? By the time the last Australian, who
happened to be Mr Wall himself, arrived (engine trouble had
delayed the gallant hop from Shoreham) Mr Gauvinier was
able to take him by the arm and show him how, with a little
care, he might still have room for the full length of his
admirable run to the wicket. This caused Mr Gauvinier the
very greatest satisfaction. Tea 7, draw 9. That was four
hours. They'd get their little game. True, the ground was a
bit confined and the autogiros had not improved the pitch:
but, good Lord! one musn't be fussy, and after all it would
be the same for both sides, and a really sporting gentleman
had returned him his boots and cap. Thus when just after five
the Australians took the field (Sam Bird squeezing between
motors had badly soiled his newly washed white umpire's
coat) and Mr Ballard and Mr McLeod reached the wickets
to bat, he felt almost at peace within and happy at the
prospect of quite a decent little game, after all.

The crowd too were in the best of spirits. They appreciated
being at such close quarters with the famous Australians,
and felt quite safe, their glass screens being Triplex and
suitably insured.

Mr Woodfull adapted his field to the new conditions, and
placed his men in a masterly manner, and with his well-
known consideration for others arranged that after each ball
his men should move one on in the small circle (more resembling Kiss-in-the-Ring perhaps than cricket) so that as many
of the spectators as possible might have the joy of close
proximity to all the great Australian players in turn.

But a large black cloud had been gathering, and as Mr
Wall, who was to open the bowling, began to walk slowly
away to count the steps of his run, a drop (and it was a large
one) fell upon his head. This caused him such surprise that
he lost count and came slowly back to the wicket: and began

once more. This time he reached the first car, which he was obliged to pass, and in it was now sitting a fair (and she was very fair) occupant. Mr Wall stopped dead. The perfectly behaved English crowd turned their heads to one side or whispered 'Will it rain?' looking upwards, and to a man thought only what would have been shouted aloud by the rude barrackers on the Hill down under. They waited in respectful silence, broken at length by a clap of thunder and a sudden downpour of rain. It was a deluge. What man in the mass had failed to stop, the weather had. Over every other trick of fate these lion-hearted fellows had prevailed: but with the weather even cricketers themselves, like Gods with stupidity, fight in vain.

No European incident occurred. Mr Hitler and Mr Stalin remained quite unperturbed; and wholly satisfied with the 'phoned apologies of the Foreign Office, each addressed their young men, without a moment's hesitation, upon the duties of Nazi and Communist citizenship respectively. The young men had heard this before many times, but drawn up in ranks, as they were, at any rate they were temporarily kept from the mischief which another would-be dictator, Mr Satan, is always anxious to find for idle hands (even when attached to Nazi or Communist wrists) to do.

So in the end all turned out really for the best in what is probably (though weather, women and what-not might conceivably be improved) the best of all possible worlds.

From Father to Sons

by SIR ARTHUR CONAN DOYLE

It is not just because I happen to be a great admirer of the Sherlock Holmes stories that their creator, Sir Arthur Conan Doyle, finds a place here. He was also a fine cricketer and, apart from playing in various Select XIs — including J. M. Barrie's Allahakbarries — was good enough for second-class cricket. On one memorable occasion he played for M.C.C. against Cambridgeshire at Lord's and returned the splendid bowling figures of seven for sixty-one!

The success of his fiction, in particular the cases of the great detective, probably prevented Sir Arthur from writing more about the game he loved. But there are indications of his fascination with the sport to be found in essays such as a study of W. G. Grace for The Strand Magazine *in 1927 and the short Holmesian tale 'The Field Bazaar'. Indeed, it has been suggested that he derived the Christian name of his famous sleuth from two cricketers who played for Nottinghamshire in the latter part of the last century — Sherwin and Shacklock — but that is pure conjecture!*

'From Father to Sons' illustrates the kind of obsession with cricket summarised by the quotation by John Arlott in the Introduction, and though the story was written half a century ago the attitudes of both generations towards the game are surely as true today as they were then.

SUPPER was going on down below and all good children should have been long ago in the land of dreams. Yet a curious noise came from above.

'What on earth—?' asked Daddy.

'Laddie practising cricket,' said the Lady, with the curious clairvoyance of motherhood. 'He gets out of bed to bowl. I do wish you would go up and speak seriously to him about it, for it takes quite an hour off his rest.'

Daddy departed upon his mission intending to be gruff, and my word, he can be quite gruff when he likes! When he reached the top of the stairs, however, and heard the noise still continue, he walked softly down the landing and peeped in through the half-opened door.

The room was dark save for a night-light. In the dim glimmer he saw a little white-clad figure, slight and supple, taking short steps and swinging its arm in the middle of the room.

'Hallo!' said Daddy.

The white-clad figure turned and ran forward to him.

'Oh, Daddy, how jolly of you to come up!'

Daddy felt that gruffness was not quite so easy as it had seemed.

'Look here! You get into bed!' he said, with the best imitation he could manage.

'Yes, Daddy. But before I go, how is this?' He sprang forward and the arm swung round again in a swift and graceful gesture.

Daddy was a moth-eaten cricketer of sorts, and he took it in with a critical eye.

'Good, Laddie. I like a high action. That's the real Spofforth swing.'

'Oh, Daddy, come and talk about cricket!' He was pulled on the side of the bed, and the white figure dived between the sheets.

'Yes; tell us about cwicket!' came a cooing voice from the corner. Dimples was sitting up in his cot.

'You naughty boy! I thought one of you was asleep, anyhow. I mustn't stay. I will keep you awake.'

'Who was Popoff?' cried Laddie, clutching at his father's sleeve. 'Was he a very good bowler?'

'Spofforth was the best bowler that ever walked on to a cricket field. He was the great Australian Bowler and he taught us a great deal.'

'Did he ever kill a dog?' from Dimples.

'No, boy. Why?'

'Because Laddie said there was a bowler so fast that his ball went frue a coat and killed a dog.'

'Oh, that's an old yarn. I heard that when I was a little boy about some bowler whose name, I think, was Jackson.'

'Was it a big dog?'

'No, no, son; it wasn't a dog at all.'

'It was a cat,' said Dimples.

'No; I tell you it never happened.'

'But tell us about Spofforth,' cried Laddie. Dimples, with his imaginative mind, usually wandered, while the elder came eagerly back to the point. 'Was he very fast?'

'He could be very fast. I have heard cricketers who had

played against him say that his yorker—that is a ball which is just short of a full-pitch—was the fastest ball in England. I have myself seen his long arm swing round and the wicket go down before ever the batsman had time to ground his bat.'

'Oo!' from both beds.

'He was a tall, thin man, and they called him the Fiend. That means the Devil, you know.'

'And *was* he the Devil?'

'No, Dimples, no. They called him that because he did such wonderful things with the ball.'

'Can the Devil do wonderful things with a ball?'

Daddy felt that he was propagating devil-worship and hastened to get to safer ground.

'Spofforth taught us how to bowl and Blackham taught us how to keep wicket. When I was young we always had another fielder, called the long-stop, who stood behind the wicket-keeper. I used to be a thick, solid boy, so they put me as long-stop, and the balls used to bounce off me, I remember, as if I had been a mattress.'

Delighted laughter.

'But after Blackham came, wicket-keepers had to learn that they were there to stop the ball. Even in good second-class cricket there were no more long-stops. We soon found plenty of good wicket-keeps—like Alfred Lyttelton and Mac-Gregor—but it was Blackham who showed us how. To see Spofforth, all india-rubber and ginger, at one end bowling, and Blackham, with his black beard over the bails waiting for the ball at the other end, was worth living for, I can tell you.'

Silence while the boys pondered over this. But Laddie feared Daddy would go, so he quickly got in a question. If Daddy's memory could only be kept going there was no saying how long they might keep him.

'Was there no good bowler until Spofforth came?'

'Oh, plenty, my boy. But he brought something new with him. Especially change of pace—you could never tell by his action up to the last moment whether you were going to get a ball like a flash of lightning, or one that came slow but full of devil and spin. But for mere command of the pitch of a ball I should think Alfred Shaw, of Nottingham, was the greatest bowler I can remember. It was said that he could pitch a ball twice in three times upon a half-crown!'

'Oo!' And then from Dimples:

'Whose half-crown?'

'Well, anybody's half-crown.'

'Did he get the half-crown?'

'No, no; why should he?'

'Because he put the ball on it.'

'The half-crown was kept there always for people to aim at,' explained Laddie.

'No, no, there never was a half-crown.'

Murmurs of remonstrance from both boys.

'I only meant that he could pitch the ball on anything—a half-crown or anything else.'

'Daddy,' with the energy of one who has a happy idea, 'could he have pitched it on the batsman's toe?'

'Yes, boy, I think so.'

'Well, then, suppose he *always* pitched it on the batsman's toe!'

Daddy laughed.

'Perhaps that is why dear old W. G. always stood with his left toe cocked up in the air.'

'On one leg?'

'No, no, Dimples. With his heel down and his toe up.'

'Did you know W. G., Daddy?'

'Oh, yes, I knew him quite well.'

'Was he nice?'

'Yes, he was splendid. He was always like a great jolly schoolboy who was hiding behind a huge black beard.'

'Whose beard?'

'I meant that he had a great bushy beard. He looked like the pirate chief in your picture-books, but he had as kind a heart as a child. I have been told that it was the terrible things in this war that really killed him. Grand old W. G.!'

'Was he the best bat in the world, Daddy?'

'Of course he was,' said Daddy, beginning to enthuse to the delight of the clever little plotter in the bed. 'There never was such a bat—never in the world—and I don't believe there ever could be again. He didn't play on smooth wickets, as they do now. He played where the wickets were all patchy, and you had to watch the ball right on to the bat. You couldn't look at it before it hit the ground and think, "That's all right. I know where that one will be!" My word, that was cricket. What you got you earned.'

'Did you ever see W. G. make a hundred, Daddy?'

'See him! I've fielded out for him and melted on a hot August day while he made 150. There's a pound or two of your Daddy somewhere on that field yet. But I loved to see it, and I was always sorry when he got out for nothing, even if I were playing against him.'

'Did he ever get out for nothing?'

'Yes, dear; the first time I ever played in his company he was given out leg-before-wicket before he made a run. And all the way to the pavilion—that's where people go when they are out—he was walking forward, but his big black beard was backward over his shoulder as he told the umpire what he thought.'

'And what *did* he think?'

'More than I can tell you, Dimples. But I dare say he was right to be annoyed, for it was a left-handed bowler, bowling round the wicket, and it is very hard to get leg-before to that. However, that's all Greek to you.'

'What's Gweek?'

'Well, I mean you can't understand that. Now I am going.'

'No, no, Daddy; wait a moment! Tell us about Bonner and the big catch.'

'Oh, you know about that!'

Two little coaxing voices came out of the darkness.

'Oh, please! Please!'

'I don't know what your mother will say! What was it you asked?'

'Bonner!'

'Ah, Bonner!' Daddy looked out in the gloom and saw green fields and golden sunlight, and great sportsmen long gone to their rest. 'Bonner was a wonderful man. He was a giant in size.'

'As big as you, Daddy?'

Daddy seized his elder boy and shook him playfully. 'I heard what you said to Miss Cregan the other day. When she asked you what an acre was you said "About the size of Daddy." '

Both boys gurgled.

'But Bonner was five inches taller than I. He was a giant, I tell you.'

'Did nobody kill him?'

'No, no, Dimples. Not a story-book giant. But a great, strong man. He had a splendid figure and blue eyes and a golden beard, and altogether he was the finest man I have ever seen—except perhaps one.'

'Who was the one, Daddy?'

'Well, it was the Emperor Frederick of Germany.'

'A Jarman!' cried Dimples, in horror.

'Yes, a German. Mind you, boys, a man may be a very noble man and be a German—though what has become of the noble ones these last three years is more than I can guess. But Frederick was noble and good, as you could see on his face. How he ever came to be the father of such a blasphemous braggart'—Daddy sank into reverie.

'Bonner, Daddy!' said Laddie, and Daddy came back from politics with a start.

'Oh, yes, Bonner. Bonner in white flannels on the green sward with an English June sun upon him. That was a picture of a man! But you asked me about the catch. It was in a Test Match at the Oval—England against Australia. Bonner said before he went in that he would hit Alfred Shaw into the next county, and he set out to do it. Shaw, as I have told you, could keep a very good length, so for some time Bonner could not get the ball he wanted, but at last he saw his chance, and he jumped out and hit that ball the most awful ker-wallop that ever was seen in a cricket field.'

'Oo!' from both boys: and then, 'Did it go into the next county, Daddy?' from Dimples.

'Well, I'm telling you!' said Daddy, who was always testy when one of his stories was interrupted. 'Bonner thought he had made the ball a half-volley—that is the best ball to hit— but Shaw had deceived him and the ball was really on the short side. So when Bonner hit it, up and up it went, until it looked as if it were going out of sight into the sky.'

'Oo!'

'At first everybody thought it was going far outside the ground. But soon they saw that all the giant's strength had been wasted in hitting the ball so high, and that there was a chance that it would fall within the ropes. The batsmen had run three runs and it was still in the air. Then it was seen that an English fielder was standing on the very edge of the field with his back on the ropes, a white figure against the black line of the people. He stood watching the mighty curve of the ball, and twice he raised his hands together above his head as he did so. Then a third time he raised his hands above his head, and the ball was in them and Bonner was out.'

'Why did he raise his hands twice?'

'I don't know. He did so.'

'And who was the fielder, Daddy?'

'The fielder was G. F. Grace, the younger brother of W. G. Only a few months afterwards he was a dead man. But he had one grand moment in his life, with twenty thousand people all just mad with excitement. Poor G. F.! He died too soon.'

'Did you ever catch a catch like that, Daddy?'

'No, boy. I was never a particularly good fielder.'

'Did you never catch a good catch?'

'Well, I won't say that. You see, the best catches are very often flukes, and I remember one awful fluke of that sort.'

'Do tell us, Daddy?'

'Well, dear, I was fielding at slip. That is very near the wicket, you know. Woodcock was bowling, and he had the name of being the fastest bowler of England at that time. It was just the beginning of the match and the ball was quite red. Suddenly I saw something like a red flash and there was the ball stuck in my left hand. I had not time to move it. It simply came and stuck.'

'Oo!'

'I saw another catch like that. It was done by Ulyett, a fine Yorkshire player—such a big, upstanding fellow. He was bowling, and the batsman—it was an Australian in a Test Match—hit as hard as ever he could. Ulyett could not have seen it, but he just stuck out his hand and there was the ball.'

'Suppose it had hit his body?'

'Well, it would have hurt him.'

'Would he have cried?' from Dimples.

'No, boy. That is what games are for, to teach you to take a knock and not show it. Supposing that—'

A step was heard coming along the passage.

'Good gracious, boys, here's Mumty. Shut your eyes this moment. It's all right, dear. I spoke to them very severely and I think they are nearly asleep.'

'What have you been talking about?' asked the Lady.

'Cwicket!' cried Dimples.

'It's natural enough,' said Daddy; 'of course when two boys—'

'Three,' said the Lady, as she tucked up the little beds.

The Day of the Duck

by JACK HOBBS

As I believe any Select XI should be allowed to have one pro-
fessional player of genuine class, I am unashamedly picking Jack
Hobbs, not only because he is one of England's greatest-ever bats-
men, whom I first heard about at my father's knee when I was still
a child, but also because he was a naturally modest man with a
marvellous sense of humour, who would have been good company—
even among the Rabbits! Jack, who was born in Cambridge and
played for the County side before joining Surrey, eventually formed
with Herbert Sutcliffe an unrivalled opening partnership for
England.

Jack's achievements as a cricketer were phenomenal, including a
record 197 centuries in first-class cricket and the highest score at
Lord's of 316 in 1926. He captained the England team, too, and
made a total of twelve centuries in Test Matches against the old
enemy, Australia. Tours 'down under' have always been tough for
England teams—but not without their funny moments. In 'The
Day of the Duck', Jack relates the kind of amusing stories from
one trip to Australia that I can imagine him telling over lunch and
tea on a gentle summer's day back home in England.

(Armstrong 100, Kelleway 80 — Total, 3 for 300...!)

I F I could remember one half of the humorous incidents
connected with the recent tour of our M.C.C. team in
Australia, I would have the ingredients for an exceedingly
bright article. At the moment I can recollect but few.

I have visited Australia on three different occasions, and
on each succeeding visit I have noticed the very rapid growth
of cricket enthusiasm. In spite of the heat, the people are
frightfully keen. They stand for whole days in sunshine
strong enough to kill. We in the field could move about
in the open, but spectators were packed. Enthusiasm was
everywhere, and the following stories will illustrate the
tremendous interest which the ordinary public took in the
'Tests' of 1920–1.

In a country centre a wedding ceremony was being
performed. Just as the question 'Will you, etc.,' was about
to be put, a telegraph messenger came in and handed a
telegram to the bridegroom. He read it and handed it to the
bride, who read it and handed it to the best man, and it went
round the whole immediate group.

'Something's happened, the wedding's off,' whispered one

49

of the onlookers. Nervously clutching the paper the officiating minister read: 'Armstrong 100, Kelleway 80; total, 3 for 300'!

'Too much public attention is given to the Test Match!' exclaimed a severe-looking gentleman on a tramcar. 'It disorganises everything. We should keep our balance and not allow sport to sway us so much.'

Presently a man jumped on the car and remarked: 'Armstrong has got his century.'

'Ah, I thought he would!' said the severe-looking gentleman.

Two workmen were making a well. One man worked on top, the other at the bottom. 'Let me know if Pellew gets his century,' said the diggist as he descended the well after lunch. By and by a paper parcel dropped on his head. He swore, and opened the parcel. He chuckled when he saw the contents by the dim candle-light—a short, straight stick and two round pebbles. Pellew had made his century!

In a restaurant was exhibited the striking sign: 'Latest cricked scores served with all meals between one and six o'clock.'

One day a client called on a firm of city solicitors. From the waiting-room he heard angry voices within.

'I tell you he didn't.'

'Oh, but he did.'

'Rot; he did it like this.'

Then, through the slightly-opened door, the client saw one of the firm pick up a walking-stick and execute a wild swipe to leg, and also accidentally sweep a water bottle off the table! He was showing how Taylor hit a certain four.

Quite a lot of cricketers who go out to Australia resent what I call the over-enthusiasm of a section of the spectators; but a public performer—and a cricketer is certainly a public performer if he relies on gate money for his living or even as a means of allowing him to play in first-class games— should not mind the criticism of the onlookers. The Australian crowds are quick in 'ragging' a cricketer, and still quicker in seeing a point out of which they can extract a certain amount of humour. I shall ever remember the fourth Test Match of our 1911–12 tour.

This game was played at Melbourne, and Wilfred Rhodes and I remained together until there were 323 on the board. Wilfred played beautifully, and the crowd showed their good humour by offering gratuitous advice to our opponents.

It was in the midst of some comical remarks that a big balloon, used for advertising purposes, with a dummy figure attached, descended almost on to the field of play.

This certainly made a break in the monotony of a long innings, and gave the 'barrackers' the chance of a lifetime, for when the dummy figure was seen a stentorian voice came from the ringside: 'Hi! Clem! (Clem Hill was the Australian captain), here's another bowler for you!'

By the way, it was during the progress of the first Test of that particular tour that I was impressed by the good nature which mostly prevails in so-called 'barracking'. This was a case of 'barracking' or 'chaffing', on the field, and happened in this way.

J. W. H. T. Douglas, Strudwick, and Mead failed to score in England's first innings, and a Sydney firm sent along a letter addressed to each, together with a hamper.

The former contained the wish that they might have better luck in the second innings, and in the latter was a fine ham for each, 'to go with the duck's egg'.

When not actually playing cricket we have always been most lavishly entertained in Australia. All sorts of entertainments were arranged for us, and there were always fun and adventure attached to them.

During the last tour the Hamilton Gun Club arranged a 'shoot' in our honour. The pick of our side were Douglas and Waddington. It was 'Waddy's' first essay at starlings, and he acquitted himself well with a strange gun in getting ten kills out of twelve birds.

Parkin competed in the 'shoot', and, as usual, caused a great amount of laughter. Even if he were to lose his bowl-

ing, Parkin should accompany every English team that tours
the Colonies. He is full of life, and with his genial smile and
a few conjuring tricks, which he has somehow mastered, is
a favourite wherever he goes.

Coming back to the matter of the 'shoot', Parkin fired
one shot, then dropped the gun, and ran back to his pals.
The fact was he'd never fired a gun before, and it kicked.
The incident caused a great deal of laughter, but the result
might have been very serious if the other barrel, which was
still loaded, had exploded.

On another occasion Mr Douglas, Parkin, Howell, and I
travelled in a car to a place called Portland. We went to visit
a friend and to take part in some sea-fishing. Our captain
and Howell went with the boat party and caught, or helped
to catch, about a hundred and fifty fish, weighing from two
to three pounds each.

Parkin and I immediately on arrival saw a tidy-sized wave,
and remembering our trip from England to Australia,
resolved to remain with the net party—that is, we helped to
haul in a net which had been taken in a sort of half-circle by
a boatman.

Parkin caused great excitement by grabbing a huge fish
and yelling for help. 'Quickly, some of you! The beggar's
got something which looks like gold in his mouth!' He
struggled with the fish while it wriggled and flapped, then
extracted a gold ring from its mouth.

The ring was duly admired, and Parkin was told to keep
it. I didn't say a word. It was one of his conjuring tricks.

In every town we visited we were invited to theatres,
fights, race-meetings, or any other form of entertainment
for which the public had to pay, but which did not cost us
any fee. We were not even called upon to hire vehicles to
carry us to these entertainments, motor-cars being sent to
fetch us from our hotels.

On one occasion Makepeace, Hearne, Dolphin, and
Howell went to the races, and managed to come back to the
hotel with some money. I learnt that Howell and Dolphin,

who were in partnership, had some extraordinarily bad luck in not returning comparatively rich men.

Just before one event Howell sent Dolphin to the Totalisator with money to put on 'No. 1' horse. Before the start, however, they discovered that they had been put on 'No. 4', owing to a mistake. There was time to change the ticket, but although Howell ragged Dolphin, nothing was done. A minute or two later 'No. 1' romped home an easy winner at huge odds.

Dolphin says he had a certain amount of respect for Howell previous to this occurrence, but now — well, he never thought a man from Edgbaston could say such awful things.

I have already written of 'remarks' made by onlookers. But one instance remains very fresh in my memory. This was at Melbourne, where the 'barrackers' were in fine form. Somehow I love these 'barrackers'. They are generally so full of humour, and they do know something about the game.

Mr Douglas was bowling with his back to the scoring-board (only one was working), and his analysis (which is always shown on Australian scoring-boards) read no wicket for some sixty runs.

Then somebody shouted, 'Why don't you go on at the other end, Johnny? You would then see your analysis.'

During the second innings of the same match Wilfred Rhodes was bowling, and had already secured two or three wickets when Douglas went into the long-field to Woolley, who was the bowler at the other end.

A man in the crowd called out suddenly, 'Here you, Johnny; Rhodes has been bowling for an hour and twenty minutes. Why don't you take the poor old man off?'

Wilfred finished up with six wickets for some thirty runs. What a great bowler he is, to be sure!

As far as the playing-grounds of Australia are concerned, it is unanimously agreed that those of Sydney and Melbourne are, without exception, the finest in the world.

But wherever one travels, however small the place, there

is always a fine cricket ground, many of them, in addition to being good from a playing point of view, being distinctly picturesque.

I mention this fact because the best wickets are made from Bulli soil, and during the recent tour we were all taken out in motor-cars through some beautiful scenery to Bulli. On arrival a gentleman of local importance made a wonderful speech of welcome, telling us that we were standing on the soil of which great quantities had been taken all over the world to make the best cricket pitches.

This, of course, was true, every cricketer knowing by repute the famous Bulli soil.

After Mr Douglas had replied to the speech, one of us happened to ask the gentleman if they played cricket in Bulli.

'Why, yes of course,' he replied. 'We've got a new concrete pitch which cost us twenty pounds, not counting the matting wicket.'

It may have appeared rude, but we could not restrain our laughter.

I was very often astonished at the wonderfully thorough knowledge of the game possessed by, seemingly, every male member of the population of the Commonwealth. Most women, too, have become expert in the technique of cricket.

However, it is said of one lady enthusiast that on Kelleway's dismissal, after making 147 in a Test Match, she expressed herself as follows: 'He has been out there running up and down the wicket for nearly a day, and now, because somebody has knocked the middle stump with a ball, he's left the ground in disgust. Hear how the crowd are encoring him! Isn't he mean not to come back?'

In the important matches, each person in the crowd seems to sit in one place, if he or she can somehow keep it, from the commencement to the finish. This is particularly noticeable in the Test Matches. When a cricket match is played, the city holds a sort of 'stop-work' meeting.

Commercial people think nothing of leaving their business for six days to witness Test Matches. They told me that if they don't come to cricket they cannot work, because their minds are on the game. And once they have secured positions on the ground, off come their coats, and they are so good-humoured that they cannot resist the temptation to 'rag' or 'barrack'.

I remember Gregory going in to bat in one Test Match, and after he had scored three, somebody shouted. 'You only want ninety-seven to make a century, Greg, old man!'

On another occasion when our bowling was collared, and seven of our side had been tried, one of the onlookers made us laugh by crying, 'Please don't put on any more bowlers, Douglas! They haven't got room on the board for them.'

The name of every bowler is put on the scoring-board, and remains there until the innings is over. During our last tour Australia was cricket mad. Men, women, and children had the disease pretty badly, and ladies sat in the sun for days to see the M.C.C. matches.

At the close of our Queensland game a lady was heard to remark: 'I've ruined my complexion for weeks to come.' She had sat for six hours on a cushion near one of the sight-screens each day.

Then she said: 'It was worth it. Jazzing will have to go by the board for a month. I simply couldn't dance with a face like this. I'll have to go into retreat.'

I was astounded at the interest shown in the last Test Match, which was at Sydney. On all days the cricket was well patronised, but on the Saturday the attendance afforded undeniable evidence that, although the rubber was won, interest was still keen.

When the luncheon adjournment took place it was thought the ground was full, but still people came, and, by squeezing a little closer, some extra sitting accommodation was secured. Then standing room became difficult to procure in the sheltered portions of the ground, and from two o'clock the people pressed outwards into the full glare of the scorching sun until there was not even standing room.

The official attendance was given as 33,608, and the receipts £3,090.

The heat did not interfere with the interest taken in the game. The ladies were, as a whole, seasonably clad, but the men were forced to put ceremony aside for the sake of comfort. Coats went first, and then vests were discarded, to be followed later by limp collars, whose places were taken by handkerchiefs, and so men sat and perspired.

The barracking was not as robust as usual, the heat being principally responsible for the languidness of the remarks, which were, on the whole, in good humour. The prime favourite with the barracking section to his last Test Match was undoubtedly Parkin, whose juggling with the ball always evoked a series of good-humoured remarks. When he once dropped the ball on reaching the crease, and with a drop-kick sent it to the wicket-keeper, the crowd simply went mad with delight. The comedy was not cricket, but the spontaneous humour of the incident was greatly appreciated.

Mr Fender's long sweater, which he wore occasionally, always caused laughter; in fact, it became known as the nightgown or the window-blind.

In one of the Test Matches our captain, J. W. H. T. Douglas, was batting somewhat on the slow side. The occasion probably demanded it, although at least one person in the crowd thought otherwise. Anyhow, this individual shouted in a loud voice, 'No wonder you couldn't win the war, Johnny.' I ought to explain that in Australia the prevailing idea is that the Australians won the war for the Allies.

I shall ever remember an incident in which Patsy Hendren was concerned, which pleased the onlookers and displeased our captain. Hendren was standing at deep third-man when a ball passed him, and he had to chase it to the boundary. In returning he made a mighty throw, but when the 'ball' bounced a few yards in front of Strudwick *it split into a hundred pieces*. As a matter of fact, when Hendren reached the boundary he picked up the ball and a *red apple*, and threw in the latter.

Hendren was always happy throughout the tour, excepting only when he was on shipboard, and then—oh! When he was at his very worst, on a particularly rough day, he looked at me with sadness in his eyes, with a green complexion, and groaned. 'Oh, Jack!' he gasped. 'Fancy! When war broke out I was thinking of joining the Navy.'

During the tour we had so many 'apple-pie' beds that I begin to feel lost without them. In one tour—not the last—on arrival at one town we were all tired out, and got to bed as soon as possible, only to find that each was 'apple-pied', a big bath-sponge, well damped, being in mine.

Of course, there is not much in this old style of joke in itself, but in this particular case the laugh was long and hearty. The next morning poor Charlie Blythe, who was one of the party, was found to be the practical joker; and what puzzled us all was the quick manner in which he played the trick, seeing that our rooms were only allocated but a short time before we retired, and it was a big hotel.

We questioned him on this point, asking, 'How did you know where each of our rooms was situated?' 'Ah,' replied Blythe, 'that's where the fun comes in. I didn't know, so had to apple-pie every bed in the hotel.'

That explained the violent and hitherto inexplicable ringing of bells on the night before.

And now for my last story. It makes an appropriate *finale* to the tales of our tour.

One morning, during the progress of the Third Test, a small boy arrived with a beautiful floral horseshoe—'For the English Eleven and its Captain, J. W. H. T. Douglas, wishing them good luck.' The gift was gratefully received, and the players appreciated the good wishes of their unknown admirer.

Douglas thought it very pretty. Strudwick, the humorist, surveyed it gravely for a moment, and then caused a roar of laughter from his comrades by remarking in a most solemn voice, 'No flowers, by request.'

A Cricketer Explains
(Strange Misfortunes on the Cricket Field)

by J. M. BARRIE

The energetic J. M. Barrie, who combined the demands of his very successful career as a novelist and dramatist with a devotion to playing cricket, would be another member of my team. His love affair with the sport is somewhat surprising considering he was born in Scotland, but he discovered the game while at school in Dumfries and was hooked for life. Barrie did not form his travelling team of writers, artists and musicians, the Allahakbarries, until he moved to London, and when fixtures for them were not available he was usually willing to turn out for local sides in the Home Counties. On one famous occasion—after his own fame was assured—he was even invited to join an Australian touring team playing an invitation game at Stanway in Gloucestershire.

Barrie began to write about the sport early in his career, when he was still a journalist in Nottingham. There he also played with a local Saturday team, and occasionally described some of their fixtures in a weekly column—though he disguised the more embarrassing moments by referring to the place as Slowcum Podger and signing himself 'Hippomenes'. Moving to London, he continued writing pieces in a similar vein for the St James's Gazette.

Although Barrie's devotion to cricket was unquestionable, he could not help seeing the funny side of the game, and several of his best stories reflect this. The next item, 'A Cricketer Explains', is another timeless excursion into the realms of cricketing obsessions, and surprisingly has never appeared in any of the author's collected works.

58

Ah, yes, but....
If only....

THIS week we concluded our engagements for the present season. I am not going to say what the name of our club is, but it begins with a C, and our averages are to be published presently in the *Dispatch*. It is this that induces me to explain in print why I have not this year come up to expectation. Going home from the office yesterday I met our club secretary on George IV Bridge, and he informed me that he was drawing up a list of averages for publication. This annoyed me a good deal, and I pointed out to him that it was not the right thing to do. Why, I said, make our private amusements public property? He chuckled at this in a way that made me hate him, and, said he, 'Why, it was you who insisted at the beginning of the season that our averages should be printed in the newspapers at the end of it.'

I detest a fellow who goes back upon what one said months ago, and I told our secretary so. He grinned again.

'I guess,' he said, 'you thought at that time that you would come out at the head of the averages instead of at the—?'

59

'So I would,' I interposed angrily, 'if it had not been for—'

'Been for what?'

'Why, for the circumstances.'

'What circumstances?'

I could not think of them at the moment, but here are the circumstances now.

Our secretary was quite right in insinuating that when the season began I was in hopes of having the best batting averages. My belief was well grounded, for I am the best bat in the eleven, as they would all admit if they did not have such a high opinion of their own batting powers.

The opening match of the season was played on our own ground, our opponents also being an Edinburgh club. I had ill-luck from the first, for the other side won the toss, and owing to an accident I failed to catch their captain in his second over. I am really a fine fielder, but in this case the ball came to me so unexpectedly that I had no time to get used to it. The sun, too, was in my eyes, and the ground being soft I slipped. Nothing could be more obvious than that I missed the ball by an accident, but for all that the spectators shouted out 'butter-fingers', and our captain sent me to field somewhere else. I was a little indignant, but 'never mind,' I said to myself, 'wait till my turn comes to bat.'

It was my first year in this club, and they had never seen me batting except when we were practising. I don't show well at practice, because there is no glory to be gained by it, but I told them that in matches I play carefully at first until I get a mastery over the bowling, after which I hit it all over the field. I was just the man they needed, so they arranged that I should go in second wicket down. H. and B. opened the batting for our side, and played very badly, the three first overs only resulting in one run. My fame as a batsman having spread among the spectators, I had a little crowd round me while B. and H. were in. I felt it my duty to criticise the batting severely.

'Well played, B.', someone cried, as B. slipped the ball for one.

'You are quite wrong,' I said. 'B. should have cut that for two or three at the least. It was a beautiful ball for cutting.'

I had a bat in my hand, and showed them how the ball should have been played.

'That was a good drive, at any rate,' someone said, as H. lifted the ball for two.

'H. did not catch the ball on the proper point of his bat,' I explained, 'or he would have driven it to the ropes. His forward play is clumsy.'

When the score had reached fifteen, H. was clean bowled.

'The ball twisted in off my pads,' he said, on returning to the pavilion.

I detest hearing a man excusing himself in this way, my own rule always being to admit a blunder if I make one.

'It was an easy ball to play,' I told him, 'if you had stepped out to it.'

W. was now in with B., and runs came slowly. I saw opportunity after opportunity missed: indeed, had I got these balls, I knew perfectly well that I would have subjected the fielders to a rare piece of leather-hunting.

'The play is tame beyond description,' I said.

'That is because the bowlers are dead on the wicket,' said H.

'I confess,' I said, 'that I see no reason for blocking because the bowling is straight. The proper way to treat these balls is to lift them over the bowler's head.'

'Now is your chance to do it, then,' said H., for while I spoke B. was caught at the wicket. The total was now thirty-one.

As I walked to the wicket there was a cheer from the crowd, for they wanted lively play. I lifted my cap in acknowledgement, and took up my position. I had never felt in better form, and as the ball left the bowler's hand I made up my mind to send it towards the pavilion. When it was half-way towards me I thought to myself, would it not be better to play a cautious game at first? This uncertainty was fatal, for before I could make up my mind the middle wicket was down.

'How's that?' cried the bowler, to whom I took an immediate dislike.

'Out,' replied the umpire, who was a most offensive fellow.

There would have been no use arguing the matter with them, so I returned to the pavilion. I did not want the cheers of the spectators; but still it struck me that their jeers following so soon after their applause showed how fickle and unreasoning they were. Our captain was just as bad, and said something about a duck's egg that I treated with silent contempt.

'You should have lifted that ball over the bowler's head,' said H.

'You are not the man to block a ball because it happens to be straight,' said B.

So they went on, as if, standing in the pavilion, they could possibly see how the ball should have been played. It is easy to brag in this way when you are watching the play from a distance. Brag of any kind, however, is detestable.

Our second match was also played in Edinburgh, though not on our own ground. This time, for a reason that I could never discover, our captain put me in sixth. It was a foolish thing to do, as I pointed out to him, for if I got well set, as would probably be the case, I would not have a chance of making a very big score before the tenth wicket fell.

'If you carry out your bat,' he said, 'I shall put you in fourth in the second innings.'

Unfortunately I did not carry out my bat. The very first ball I got I hit for two, and the captain shouted out, 'Well hit, sir'. After that I got no balls for some time, the man who was in along with me getting them all. This was to be regretted for the sake of our club, for he blocked ball after ball that I could have sent away for two and three. I was amazed to see him play so gingerly when the bowling was so weak.

At last my turn came again. The ball was breaking from the off when I drew it beautifully. I did not see where it went to, but the other batsman, B., shouted 'Run,' and I ran.

'Another,' he cried, beginning to run again.

My idea was that I had hit the ball, and I thought I saw cover-point flinging it to the wicket-keeper.

'Go back,' I shouted to B.

'It's an easy run,' he panted, for being quicker sighted than I he knew that I had hit the ball to leg.

There was a yelling of advice from the pavilion, but I would not run, and the result was that B. was run out before he could get back to his wickets. With an unreasonableness that made me feel sorry for him, he put all the blame on my head, and came dancing up to me in a passion.

'You ass!' he cried.

I smiled.

'What do you mean by running me out in this way?' he growled, looking as if he could strike me.

'It was your own fault,' I said.

'Not a bit of it. There was abundance of time.'

'I thought I cut the ball to cover-point.'

'What! You thought you had hit to leg! Well, you are a curiosity in cricket.'

So he went off fuming, as men of his type do. The proper course in the circumstances, of course, would have been to admit good-naturedly that the fault was his own. But he is not enough of a gentleman to do that.

I had now scored three in all, and felt that I was beating the bowling. No cricketing reader requires to be told that there are occasions when a batsman feels that he is in magnificent form. Then his eye is quick, all nervousness has worn off, and he is in a condition for rapid scoring. Those were now my feelings, and I daresay the 'out' side could read them in my face. At all events, I saw their captain send one or two of them further away from the wickets. Either he was frightened that they were not safe in close proximity to me, or he thought there was a chance of a catch at the ropes.

The next ball I got I drove vigorously, but the bowler stopped it. If he had been in his proper place it would have passed him, but he was a restless fellow, who could not stand still. His next ball was a 'yorker', and I missed it. It struck my leg.

'How's that?' someone cried.

'Out,' said the umpire.

'Who is out?' I asked.

'You are,' said the wicket-keeper.

'Out! How can I be out?'

'Lbw,' said the umpire.

This was a little too much.

'Do you mean to say,' I said, 'that my leg is in front of the wicket? Good gracious man, come and look.'

'That won't do,' said the wicket-keeper.

'What won't do?'

'None of your blarney.'

'I insist,' I said, 'upon knowing what you mean.'

'Why, that is not where your leg was when the ball hit it.'

'I haven't moved it an inch.'

'You've moved it half a yard.'

'Next man,' shouted the umpire.

In the whole course of my cricketing experience I have known nothing more infamous. I can only conclude that they saw they would never get me out by fair means and so determined to dispose of me foully. The worst of it was that I got no sympathy from my own side. I wanted them to stop the match, but they said 'fudge'. When I insisted with the captain that my leg was not in front of the wickets, he said, 'That is what they all say when they are out lbw,' implying that I was trying to cheat. I, who pride myself on nothing so much as my honesty. I asked him fiercely if that was what he meant, and he replied that it was. This so disgusted me that I went away and sat by myself on the fence.

In the second innings I was given out caught by the wicket-keeper, though I never touched the ball. It is not my intention to describe my misfortunes step by step, for that would occupy too much space, and besides, one match was very like another. All through the season I never got a chance of showing what I could do, because just when I was settling down to a big score I was put out. The games on our own ground I did not do well in, because somehow I never feel in good form on our own ground, while on other grounds I cannot play well because I am not used to them. It was my miserable luck, too, always to get difficult balls to play when I went in. The other men on our side got balls I could have hit out of the grounds, but no such balls ever came to me. Just because I never made big scores, too, our captain argued that I was not a good player, and he took to putting me in last man. Three times I was put out lbw, most unfairly, twice I was run out entirely through the fault of others, and I was caught four times by fielders who were standing in the wrong place. The luck, indeed, has been hopeless against me all through the year, and I have never had a chance of distinguishing myself.

Fuji Kawa: The Cricket Star

by HESKETH PRICHARD

Hesketh Prichard was a larger-than-life character who played cricket with the same swashbuckling style that he wrote fiction, and would be welcome in any side of mine. Born in India just six weeks after his father had died of typhoid, Hesketh was brought home to England by his mother. He quickly displayed a talent for sport. Discovered as a fast bowler while still at school, he was taken on the staff of Hampshire C.C. and played for the side from 1899 to 1913. From 1903 to 1905 he also appeared in the annual Gentleman v. Players fixtures.

But even cricket did not totally satisfy Hesketh, and he started travelling the world. For a time he was a noted big-game hunter in the Americas and Europe, and even led an expedition to Patagonia. Soon after this he began to draw on his travel experiences to write books as well as serials for a number of popular journals. For Pearson's Magazine he created a very successful series about a villainous bandit named Don Q, and for the same publication also provided several stories featuring a cricket professional named Smith, which were spiced with his own exploits and humour.

A big, ebullient man whose good nature was legendary in cricketing circles, Hesketh joined the Army during the First World War and rose to become a major. He died, tragically, when only forty-five after enduring fourteen operations to cure an obscure blood disease. Something of his humour and inventive imagination will be found in this next story, in which a Japanese—typically of the race which seems to have become supreme master of technology—comes up with a revolutionary idea for the playing of cricket as well.

Fuji Kawa, a most capable young Japanese gentleman, had been in England a little over two years. He had been sent by a progressive and enlightened Government intent upon railway expansion to investigate and report upon the best types of triple expansion engines and tubular boilers, and he worked in the drawing offices and shops of the West Central Railway Company, Limited.

He was a many-sided man, and of a most original and inventive turn of mind. Witness the ingenious way in which he adapted the turbine type of marine engine to the needs of railway locomotion. In one way or another it was his habit to improve almost everything he was concerned in. Had he not been in the very first flight as an engineer, he might have made a handsome income on the music-hall stage as a juggler. He could draw and paint beautifully, and was seldom at a loss for new and luminous ideas about any subject you might touch upon, from chess to canary-breeding.

Yet there was nothing very striking in his appearance. He was simply a little brown-faced man, with high cheek-bones

67

and coal-black hair. Almost the only thing he could not do was to pronounce the letter 'l'. Otherwise his English was practically perfect.

One bright April evening Fuji Kawa turned up on the ground of the West Central Railway Cricket Club. He stood smoking his pipe behind the net, watching the batsmen with an air of abstraction.

The captain was kneeling near him, putting on his pads.

'Ever played cricket, Fudgey?'

'Yes. I prayed a bit with some Engrish boys in Japan.'

'Ah! Now that's where you won't be able to make any of those improvements you are so fond of!'

'I don't know,' said Fuji Kawa, quietly; 'I rike my way of batting better than yours.'

'Bless the man! Whatever will he say next?'

Nevertheless, when the captain's innings was over, he came back and, tossing over to Fuji Kawa the pads he had just taken off, shouted to him in merry scorn:—

'Here! Put 'em on, Fudgey. I want to see you reform English cricket!'

Fuji Kawa smiled and said nothing; then he put the pads on.

When his turn came his proceedings were of an extraordinary character. Placing one foot on each side of the block-hole, he faced the bowler full-fronted, in much the same way as a wicket-keeper does. His position suggested croquet rather than cricket.

The majority laughed at him and seemed to anticipate an exquisite piece of fooling. Those who knew him, and had learnt that there was generally an excellent reason for everything he did, watched attentively.

For the first few balls the bowlers were not serious. Fuji Kawa played the straight ones with ease and thumped a long-hop to leg with careless vigour. Then they began to think there might be something in the man after all, and tried their best to get him out. Fuji Kawa's stumps remained intact, and he glanced many a good ball behind the wicket, both to leg and off.

'Here, Stokes,' cried one of the bowlers to the ruddy professional, 'take my ball. Come and get this beggar out.'

Stokes bowled his best and fastest. He was a really good bowler, and often got a wicket with an express delivery which pitched inches to the off and took the leg-stump. However, he made no more impression on Fuji Kawa's defence than the others had done.

Then he tried the off-theory. The only result was that Fuji Kawa took to slipping his left hand down the handle below the right, and repeatedly hit him left-handed square past cover-point.

'I rike a bat frat on both sides,' he explained. Of course there was chaff for Stokes. How did he expect to keep up his name if he got smacked about all over the field by the first foreigner he bowled at? Whereupon the worthy Stokes, whose misfortune it was to be somewhat short-tempered, threw down his ball, saying it wasn't cricket.

'Let them as talks loudest get him out,' he declaimed, with no little heat. 'I knows 'ow to bowl to a right-'ander and I knows 'ow to bowl to a left-'ander. But thump my weskit if anybody can bowl to a right-'ander and a left-'ander at the same bloomin' time.'

And he walked away, with intense dignity.

'Can you play at Barton next Saturday, Fudgey?' asked the captain.

'If you rike,' said Fuji Kawa.

The West Central were not doing well at Barton. The home team had declared their innings closed at 148 for six wickets. The visitors had seven men out for sixty-one, and there was still half an hour to play.

Fuji Kawa was in next. Several disconsolate batsmen sitting in the pavilion watched him anxiously as he walked to the wickets.

He took guard, and then faced the bowler in his peculiar way.

That worthy hesitated, and looked as if about to accuse him of deliberately wasting time.

'Now, then,' cover-point exclaimed, 'take time off umpire!'

'I am quite ready,' said Fuji Kawa.

'I can't bowl at him like that,' said the bowler to the umpire; 'where are the wickets?'

'Never mind, my boy. You'll soon hit his leg,' was the significant whisper.

The first ball was a good one, and Fuji Kawa pushed it gently back to the bowler, without moving either foot. The next was shorter. He turned on it like a lion, and hooked it round to square-leg for four, in a way that Ranjitsinhji himself could not have excelled. The third ball was meant for a yorker, but Fuji Kawa skipped nimbly down the pitch and got another four to leg. Off the last ball of the over he scored a neat two behind the wicket.

'I can't make him out!' said the bowler to the Barton captain as the fielders crossed over.

A bye brought Fuji Kawa to the other end. Off the fast bowler he immediately took two two's and a three to fine long-leg.

The Barton spectators, who had been merry while the wickets were falling fast, watched in silent perplexity. The captain began to alter his field. Two men were taken out of the slips and placed square and deep on the leg-side. Cover-point was ordered to betake himself to fine long-leg.

Fuji Kawa was ready for this move. He began to slip his left hand below the right and to hit left-handed to leg through the place cover-point had just vacated. Three times in succession he made a four by this stroke. The hundred was hoisted, and both bowlers were showing signs of temper. Neither of them had succeeded in hitting Fuji Kawa's leg. The West Central men thought the game was saved, and were getting jubilant. Then the other batsman made a bad stroke and was caught at cover. Eight wickets were down for 105, and there was ten minutes to play.

The fielders were told to scatter themselves equally all round the wickets and look out for chances. Fuji Kawa placed almost every ball between them with the greatest ease, and scored either two or four, keeping the bowling almost entirely to himself. The total mounted by leaps and bounds to 140, when a rising ball hit his glove and dropped on his foot.

''S that?' yelled an infuriated fieldsman.

The mendacious umpire raised his hand.

'Out? How out?' asked Fuji Kawa.

'Leg-before.'

'Reg-before? Off my grove?'

'Good-bye, mister,' said cover-point, with a broad grin; 'you've got to go.'

Fuji Kawa stroked his nose reflectively and went. The last man came in, trembling in every fibre of his body; but he safely negotiated the rest of the over. Then the church clock chimed half-past six and the game was drawn.

Fuji Kawa sat in the captain's room that evening, discussing the match over a pipe.

'We should have won, Fudgey, if you hadn't been swindled out. Still, I can't think what made you take to such a rummy way of batting. Isn't it dangerous with fast bowling?'

'Not more dangerous than wicket-keeping, I think.'

The captain told him that what passed for fast bowling in local cricket was only called medium in county games.

Whereupon Fudgey asked whether there was a really fast bowler engaged on the county ground. On being told there was one, he took down the address of the Wessex secretary.

On the Monday evening Fuji Kawa appeared at the county nets and faced the fast bowler. After being hit twice on the thigh and once in the stomach he found the Wessex professional's pace was too great for him to be able to play a good length ball without moving his feet; but as he became accustomed to the new conditions his natural genius seemed to come to his aid and he began to play forward, first right-handed and then left-handed, in a style that was a modification of the ordinary one.

The great man slanged his methods energetically, as was only natural, but did not get him out.

On three Saturdays out of the next four Fuji Kawa made a century for the West Centrals. His fame began to be noised abroad throughout the length and breadth of Wessex.

The *Wessex Evening Pioneer* had a paragraph in its weekly cricket notes, stating that it might be worth the while of the county committee to keep an eye on the batting of a young Japanese gentleman in the service of the West Central Railway Company. His method, it was true, was what might be termed revolutionary; even more so, in fact, than that of Ranjitsinhji himself. But the fortunes of western county cricket had been for some years steadily on the wane. Enterprise must be looked for; and the committee could not afford to overlook the claims of a batsman who averaged nearly two hundred in local matches.

The county captain warmly advocated Fuji Kawa's claims to a place in the team. But the committee told him that, although they attached very great weight to his recommendations, they felt unable to play a batsman whose methods were so unorthodox. He replied that if he wasn't going to have a voice in the selection of the team he led they might go to Hanover and get their whiskers singed. Further, they might find another captain at their earliest convenience.

As desirable captains were hard to find in Wessex the committee caved in under protest, and Fuji Kawa was given a trial on the home ground against Yorkshire.

The Yorkshiremen batted first and made 205. At the end of the first day's play Wessex were out for a paltry ninety-nine, Fuji Kawa having been bowled between his legs for seven. It did not occur to the northern cracks that they need make a big score in the second innings. Their next match was at the other end of the country, and they would all rather sleep in bed than in the train. They hoped to finish the match in two days and travel in comfort on the third. Care in such matters is well repaid before the end of a long season. After luncheon on Tuesday they sent Wessex in to make 290 to win. Everybody thought this a hopeless task against the best bowling in England.

This time Fuji Kawa was sent in first. He began very carefully, and the score crept up to thirty before his partner was magnificently caught at extra cover. Fuji Kawa was joined by his captain, a young giant with tremendous driving powers.

Nevertheless, the little man began to score three runs for every one that his partner made. Throwing restraint to the winds, he hit all round the wicket with wonderful confidence. Glances, hooks, and forward push-strokes almost seemed to jostle each other on their way to the boundary. It did not seem to matter in the least how the field was altered. Fuji Kawa's strokes were nearly always placed between the men. After an hour's batting he completed his hundred, the total being only 140.

The crowd cheered rapturously.

'Dash my wig,' cried one enthusiast to his friend, 'if he goes on like this we shall win. *Win!* D'ye hear, Tom?'

And he thumped the other violently on the back.

'Drop it, you silly juggins, and watch the game. Ain't they crowding in?'

News of what was going on had penetrated into the town. The ring of spectators, often incomplete, was gradually becoming three or four deep.

Fuji Kawa never turned a hair. He started for his second hundred with the utmost composure. Two hundred was telegraphed before the captain was neatly stumped. Yorkshire found themselves facing the prospect of an utterly unexpected defeat.

The next batsman was a slow scorer, but Fuji Kawa continued to make runs at the same tremendous pace. The curious thing was that he never seemed to be hitting hard and always kept the ball down; but the fielders had to be so much spread out for his multitudinous strokes that he always seemed to be able to find the intervals between them. The policy of 'nine men on the off' was futile when Fuji Kawa was at the wicket. Seldom did he fail to score a couple of boundaries in any over. The Wessex spectators had not given vent to such roars of delight for many a long year.

The bowling was repeatedly changed, but the rate of scoring was kept up. Shortly before five o'clock a tumult of applause, louder and more prolonged than ever, greeted the little Japanese. He had broken record by scoring 200 in his first county match. The ring had the appearance of effervescing with hats and sticks.

Another four to Fuji Kawa and the game was won.

The players made for the pavilion at a gallop, but their effort was of no avail. With one mind the crowd charged upon them from all sides, laughing, cheering, shouting, and madly throwing into the air everything that they could lay their hands upon. Each man and boy was wildly determined to get a close view of the wonderful little Japanese. Eventually he was carried into the pavilion on the shoulders of the Yorkshire players.

The police were powerless to make that crowd go. The people thronged in front of the building clamouring for a speech, but as nobody kept silent there was very little chance of Fuji Kawa's being heard. He came out on the balcony and repeatedly raised his cap. Again and again was the cheering renewed. Never had any cricketer so suddenly leaped into the very heyday of popularity. By none was he more heartily congratulated than by the Yorkshire captain.

Next day a prominent London daily gave tongue as follows:

Much has lately been written and said concerning the rapidly advancing tide of progress in the Land of the Rising Sun. We have been told repeatedly of the remarkable adaptability of the Japanese race for assimilating the knowledge of the West and benefiting by European

inventions and enlightenment. Very few people, however, could have imagined yesterday that the inborn
genius of a Japanese gentleman would have surmounted
the difficulties inseparable from a novice in county
cricket, and broken all English records for a first appearance by scoring 204 not out. We are told that his method
is absolutely original, and that he uses a bat which is
flat on both sides. No doubt this is a daring innovation;
but it is only what might have been expected from a
member of such a virile and ingenious race. Should
his success continue, we fully anticipate that a band of
imitators will spring up, to multiply the troubles of the
modern bowler. In that case we look for a storm of
protest and much newspaper correspondence. It is rash,
however, to venture upon prediction, unless possessed
of knowledge. We can only speculate as to what the
future will bring forth.

Fuji Kawa's success throughout the month of June was
consistent and no less remarkable. Every week he headed
the *Sportsman's* list of averages, with a record that gradually
ascended from 150 towards 200. His portrait began to be
enclosed in packets of cigarettes and thrown on the screen
in places of entertainment, receiving applause as enthusiastic
as that bestowed on the presentment of the German
Emperor. By the end of the month he had scored more than
two thousand runs and had only been dismissed eleven times.

His place in the Gentlemen's team for the Lord's match
against the Players became absolutely secure. Wessex, instead
of being at the bottom of the list of counties, stood in the
second place, having been only once defeated.

It was the second day of the great match. Every inch of
space at Lord's was taken up. Thirty thousand people had
been refused admission at the turnstiles for want of room.

The Players had stayed in all the first day, making 480
runs.

'I don't think the Gentlemen will get so many,' said a man in the crowd.

'Give me ten to one that Fudgey don't mike more than that hisself, and I'll tike yer,' said his neighbour.

'Shut up, you idiot!' said the first speaker, clapping his hands as the professionals came out, tossing the ball from one to another.

Fuji Kawa and a batsman of hitherto unrivalled fame followed after a brief interval, receiving a tremendous ovation. His partner took the first ball and scored a three to leg. The next was a yorker of terrific pace, and hit Fuji Kawa on the ankle. There was a unanimous confident appeal. The umpire's right hand twitched at his side. Then he slowly shook his head, thinking he 'was not quite sure it would have hit the sticks'. The crowd gasped with relief, and gave vent to their feelings by cheering lustily.

As it turned out, no decision ever given by an umpire on the cricket field was more momentous than this one. Throughout the whole of that long, hot day the two batsmen defied every bowler on the Players' side. When the tired fielders at last had respite from their labours, Fuji Kawa had made 705!

The total was 1048 for no wicket.

The scene that took place when the stumps were drawn is said to have been beyond description.

The Gentlemen declared their innings closed without batting on the third day, and won by an innings and 300.

At the end of the season Fuji Kawa had attained the unprecedented aggregate of 5054 runs, averaging 172.

Then the newspaper correspondence began to rage in deadly earnest. The county captains held a meeting in December. Resolutions were passed—the Wessex captain alone dissenting—recommending the M.C.C. to amend the laws of the game so as to forbid Fuji Kawa's unorthodox methods.

However, they might have saved themselves the trouble. Fuji Kawa went back to Japan in January. He is now devoting himself heart and soul to the construction of railways and locomotives in that progressive land. People say he is doing magnificently.

The proposed alterations in the laws of cricket were not made, and never will be, unless another Fuji Kawa turns up.

But that is not likely.

Five Short Legs

by A. G. MACDONELL

A. G. Macdonell, for anyone who needs reminding, is the author of England, Their England, *published in 1933. Said to be the funniest book ever written about the English, it contains what many consider the funniest account of a village cricket match. The book has rather overshadowed Archie Macdonell himself, which is a pity because he was a lively, wholehearted man who loved cricket and would be an asset to any Select XI. J. C. Squire, another writer and Archie's close friend (to whom* England, Their England *is dedicated because it was his team, the Invalids, that inspired the cricketing chapter) once said of him that he was 'a cricketer who might not make many runs, but would chase the ball with vigour and would certainly heighten any team's morale.' Surely no side is complete without such a chap!*

Archie, like J. M. Barrie, was born in Scotland, but did not discover the delights to be found at the crease until he began his education at Winchester. Thereafter he interrupted his literary career every summer to play for a number of teams and introduced the subject into several of his books. Much as I like England, Their England *and its chapter on cricket, it is one of the most anthologised of stories and I prefer to use something rather less well known for this book. Indeed, the following story—a chapter from another of Archie's novels,* How Like an Angel—*may well be unknown to many readers as it has long been out of print.*

The tale concerns Hugo Seeley, a film star and aspiring cricketer, who develops a lethal but effective form of leg-stump bowling with a 'trap' of five short legs! As a result he finds himself selected to play for a beleaguered England side in a Test Match—with the most hilarious results. Archie's inspiration is clear enough, and of it the cricket historian Alan Ross has commented, 'It is perhaps the only good thing that resulted from the unhappy "leg-theory" incidents of the 1932–3 tour of Australia.' I also happen to be fond of this story because Hugo's cricketing odyssey begins in the Suffolk countryside, not much farther than a good six hit from where I live.

THERE is peace to be found in the county of Suffolk, and for a couple of weeks Hugo found it. The nightmare life of London dropped away in a moment, just as real nightmares drop away when the sleeper awakens out of darkness into the sunlight. Felida and Mr Dowley, and the terrifyingly unscrupulous Dope, receded into a dim obscurity. The hue-and-cry for Michael Seeley had died down the instant Aurora claimed the prize, and the great honest heart of the British Public was concentrating now upon the exploits of the Borealian cricket eleven, which was touring the country. The lustre of the high-dive into the Welsh Harp had already been dimmed by the innings of 340 not out which a young gentleman from Kicking Mule Gulch, Murrumbridgee County, Borealia, had scored in three hours against the unfortunate citizens of Glamorgan, Britain, and the roseleaf curve of Felida's lips was rapidly fading before the sensation at Nottingham when the Might of England (a technical journalistic expression for eleven cricketers) was overthrown in a single innings by the redoubtable Wheatstalks.

80

And so poor Hugo found some peace in Suffolk at last. It was a conclusive proof of his worn and battered condition of body and mind that he should have selected for his retreat one of those counties which Uncle Eustace so heartily despised. If Hugo had been his normal self he would never have dreamt of staying, deliberately, of his own free will, in a county which was not good enough to compete in the First-Class County Cricket Championship, but only pottered about in the Minor Championship. But he was so tired that he did not care. And any faint twinge of conscience that he may have felt, was softened by the fact that although he went into Suffolk every day, he slept every night in Saffron Walden in the First-Class County of Essex.

It was early June, and Suffolk is very lovely in early June. It is a county of corn-growing, rich red ploughland in the spring, and in the summer rolling fields of ripening grain. The kindly earth is full of promise for the harvest. The villages are small and the farmhouses far between; here and there a derelict windmill stands in the summery haze, with a brave old defiance against all modernity. And everywhere are the great parish churches that might easily be taken for small cathedrals, splendid survivals of the days when East Anglia was a humming little world of cloth-workers, when the villages of Kersey and Woolsey sold their wares in markets that lay within sound of the carillon of the Beffroi of Bruges, when Worsted was a prosperous townlet of Norfolk, and the Cloth Hall at Ypres was symbolical of other things than savage destruction.

Hugo wandered in a dream through the long village of Long Melford, past the old Bull Inn to the Green and the stately church beyond it, with its stained glass and its painted frescoes in the Clopton Chapel. He woke up for a moment or two when he found himself in the tiny church at Acton gazing down at the brass effigy of Sir Robert de Bures, the second of the four great brasses of England, lying there in its chain-mail as Sir Robert himself must have lain 630 years ago. And near the armed knight was the brass of Alice de

Bryan, a widow lady, in a simple gown. He went to Clare, a small, sleepy, tired village that has given its name to a Cambridge College and a county of Ireland, to the Dukedom of Clarence and the Clarenceux King-of-Arms. And from Clare he drifted through the magic lanes to Stoke-by-Nayland with its rose-pink church tower, and the busy little town of Sudbury, birthplace of Gainsborough and scene of the Eatanswill election, and to East Bergholt where Constable was born, and so wandering he came past many churches till he came to the greatest of them all, the dark grey, dominant splendour of the church at Lavenham.

It seemed to Hugo to be a land that has been forgotten by Progress. He saw no gangs of housebreakers picking away at the Tudor Hall at Melford, to replace it with blocks of flats. He saw no tearing down of moated granges to make way for offices in concrete and steel, to be filled with glass furniture and overworked typists. Development, that blessed word which used to mean only the change in a photographic negative from absence of visible picture to presence of visible picture, and which now means change from ancient loveliness to modern hideousness, had not yet reached Suffolk. This, felt Hugo, was the England that Uncle Eustace had known and loved, the England of beer and Queen Victoria and Doctor W. G. Grace. No one in Suffolk would throw him out of aeroplanes. No one in Suffolk would stick revolvers into his ribs. No one in Suffolk had ever heard of Tabriz in Northern Persia, home-town of Arfa-ed-Dovleh.

So Hugo wandered in the enchanted land, and leant on stiles, and smelt the honeysuckle and gazed at the sheets of brass where the buttercups glittered beneath the willows, and talked to innkeepers. He drank the beer of Greene King, whose plaque, like a bas-relief of Lucca della Robbia, on the walls of many inns, is a sure proof to the thirsty wayfarer that good beer is obtainable within. He learnt, among other strange bits of lore, that people only go to Clare to die, and even at that they are not very successful, and that at Lavenham people only get out of bed on Thursdays. He learnt

that kittens which are born when the brambles are out are
weakling kittens, whereas kittens which are born when the
whitethorn is in bloom are rare little devils for the mice. He
watched a man making brooms for sale in Saffron, a man
whose great-grandfather had made brooms for sale in Saffron, and he found an old lady who was making a smock.
But who was likely to wear the smock was not so easily
discoverable.

   And on wet afternoons Hugo strolled, awe-struck,
through the rooms of the Saffron Walden Museum and gazed
at the skeletons of long-forgotten mastodons, and the strange
fauna of long-melted glaciers, and the trophies of many a
long-dead Anglo-Indian colonel. Hugo never mastered, nor
could he find anyone to help him to master, the connection
between the bones of prehistoric mammalia and the sweet
cornlands of English Suffolk. But there they are, room after
room of them, jostling and jumbling each other so closely
that is is often difficult to distinguish between the bones of
the yak which Smithers Sahib shot near Gilgit in '84, and
the bones of the rat which Smithers Sahib, then of course a
much older and more highly seasoned man, strongly denied
having seen on the floor of the Officers' Mess in Amballa in
'99. But come yaks, come rats, it is all one to Saffron
Walden. Few of the citizenry above the school leaving-age
visit that dread mausoleum. The town rests content upon its
bulb of Saffron-crocus which was brought by the palmer
from Jerusalem, concealed in a hollow in his palmer's staff,
the very first bulb of the coveted yellow dye to be smuggled
into England.

One morning, a June morning, a morning of birdsong and
hedge-scent and the far-off cries of haymakers, Hugo was
drifting along an enchanted lane. Clematis was flowering in
the thorn-bushes and the edges of the lane were thick with
the flower that the English call ladies'-lace and Socrates called
hemlock. There was even a faint touch of dust in the air,
and in these days you have to be a long way from rushing

cars, and tar-macadam roads, and concrete racing-tracks, and A.A. Scouts, to get a touch of dust in the air. The corn was beginning to turn from dark jade to pale lemon, and there was no wind. Bees and butterflies wandered hither and thither so slowly that it seemed as if they thought their span of life was eternity and not a little hour.

Suddenly Hugo stopped. A sound had come through the belt of beechwoods, a staccato sound, a crisp, brisk click. There it was again. And again, click.

It was unmistakeable. Hugo had never heard it before, the real authentic sound of willow upon stitched leather. But he had often enough heard the sound of palm-wood upon a primitive ball of coconut fibre with goatskin stretched round it, and he knew that beyond the belt of beechwoods a game of cricket was in progress.

A game of cricket! Kalataheira sprang before his eyes. Scarlet parrakeets flapped across the Suffolk corn; tom-toms were beating in the vestry of that old stone church with the rose-pink brick tower; the murmurous lapping of small waves upon coral came whispering through the woods. And there, in the enchanted lane, stood the ghost of Uncle Eustace, shaking a finger and talking. What was he saying? The words were almost audible, those oft-repeated, well-remembered words, 'If the batsman shows a tendency to draw away from the wicket, put three men on the leg-side and send him down a fast yorker on the leg-stump.' Dear Uncle Eustace, with your great beard and your deep, strong laugh, and your simple mind. Get the man out in any way you can, so long as you keep within the letter of the law. Dear Uncle Eustace, that was the fifth of your five gospels. Hugo smiled a gentle, reflective smile. The old boy did not seem to know very much about women, but he did know about cricket.

Click! There it was again. Hugo began to hurry. It was only half-past eleven, and the match probably had not yet begun. If he was quick, he might not miss a single ball, he, brought up to cricket from infancy, and never yet a player or a spectator in any match. He broke into a run, and soon came round the corner of the beeches on to that loveliest of English sights, a country-house cricket ground, surrounded by trees, in the sunlight. The wickets were pitched, the outfield was mown, the sight-screens were sheets of white against the trees. Rows of deck-chairs were filled with shimmering summer-frocks and pale silk stockings, and surmounted with gay dragon-fly parasols, and in front of them the players themselves were practising, some batting, some bowling, others throwing catches to each other. Hugo with a thrill recognised the blazers of the Foresters, the Hogs, the Dumplings, the Stragglers, I Zingari, the Nomads, and many another Joseph's coat.

He crossed a buttercup-meadow until he reached the fence of the cricket field itself, and then he leant upon it and looked across at the beautiful, shimmering kaleidoscope. A quarter to twelve struck upon an invisible clock. Hugo wondered when they were going to begin. The practising was slackening off, and the men in flannels were clustering in small groups and talking. Then a telegraph-boy arrived with a telegram, and there was a lot of shouting and running to and fro. Still the game did not begin. Finally the captains tossed and one side came out to field. It consisted of eight men in white flannels, a gardener's boy in corduroys and a grey flannel shirt, a chauffeur in blue breeches and black, shiny leggings, and another man in flannels who followed a few minutes later amid shouts of 'I'll relieve you when you like, Jim.' This was obviously a substitute lent to the fielding side by the batting side.

By a curious chance the very first ball of the match was hit sharply to the boundary almost exactly where Hugo was watching. In order to save a long run for one of the fieldsmen, Hugo picked it up—the first real cricket-ball which he had ever handled—and flicked it full pitch exactly into the wicket-keeper's hands with the effortless ease of one who has been accustomed to bring down a humming-bird with a coconut at eighty yards range, five times out of six.

Two overs later the same thing happened, and a tall middle-aged man, wearing an Eton Rambler scarf and an air of authority, strolled across the ground between two overs and called out to Hugo:

'You a cricketer, sir?'

'Well—er—er—'

'Care to turn out for us?' went on the man. 'We're three short.'

Hugo was enthralled. To play cricket—a real game—with real cricketers—if only Uncle Eustace had been there to see. And how Uncle René would have smiled.

'They'll fix you up with kit at the house,' said the Rambler. 'Tell them I sent you. Vernon is the name.'

'I'd love to,' exclaimed Hugo enthusiastically.

'Good man,' said the other, and he went back to his place.

A quarter of an hour later, Hugo, feeling very self-conscious and very proud, was standing in an alert position at extra-cover-point.

There was plenty of fielding to be done, for the opening pair of batsmen soon found their form, and it turned out that two of the three missing players were the star bowlers of their team. The score mounted rapidly and Hugo was kept busy. But Uncle Eustace's teaching, and those laborious hours of practice on the scented evenings by the lagoon, bore fruit on this Suffolk playing-ground, and Hugo won many little tributes of applause by the brilliance of his picking-up and the lightning accuracy of his throwing.

At one o'clock play was stopped for luncheon, with the score standing at 131 for no wickets. Mr Vernon walked agross to Hugo and asked him his name. Hugo hesitated. If he said Smith and someone recognised him as the film star, it would lead to awkward explanations. On the other hand, now that the excitement and the hue and cry had died down, there could be no harm in boldly taking advantage of the prestige of the name of Seeley on an ephemeral occasion like this. Hugo therefore replied firmly, 'My name is Seeley.' He was rather surprised, and a little disappointed, that the Eton

Rambler registered no sign of ever having heard the name before. Nor did the other members of the team to whom he was introduced. Among the ladies, however, there was a most gratifying buzz of recognition. Several fair ones, who had been asleep in their deck-chairs for some time, awoke suddenly. Others instantly abandoned the knitting or sewing upon which they were relying to pull them through the tedium of watching their 'men-folk' at their dull and stupid game. Others, again, shut their novels hastily, while only a group of three or four young ladies of about seventeen years of age paid no attention to him, but continued to stare with rapt adoration upon the two incoming batsmen, both of whom, it appeared, had played cricket for Middlesex.

The enthusiasm with which the ladies clustered round Hugo at first puzzled Mr Vernon and his elegant colleagues, for they were not accustomed to being ignored in this way on their majestic return to the luncheon-tent, but when Hugo's identity was revealed to them, they became extremely sulky. It was true that the fellow's fielding had been astonishingly brilliant, but that was just the sort of monkey-trick which these fellows were taught in their profession. Just like doing acrobatics on the balcony of the Ritz and jumping out of aeroplanes and so on. In a very few minutes Mr Vernon and his colleagues and his opponents were feeling like the Guardsmen in *Patience* who found that in spite of their 'uniforms handsome and chaste the peripatetics of long-haired aesthetics are very much more to their taste.'

Hugo, however, was delighted. The excitement of his first match, the applause which he had won, the strength of the home-brewed ale, the beauty of the countryside, and the unaffected admiration of so many charming ladies, not so beautiful perhaps as Felida but far less sophisticated, all mounted to his head and made him forget his natural shyness. One or two slightly *risqué* bits of repartee, rather in the style of Uncle René, brought peals of silvery giggling and numerous dark and heavy scowls. Hugo began to wonder if he might not find some charmer at this very table who

would masquerade as Aurora in a Brighton hotel, and scruti-
nised each of his immediate neighbours in a way which they
found enchanting and the cricketers licentious. But they all
looked so very simple and gay and innocent that he soon
abandoned the notion. These pretty creatures of the country
were very different from the experienced, self-reliant women
of a great city like London. Hugo felt that it would be a
crime to make temporary love to any of them. It would
leave behind a broken heart and a blasted life. He directed
his attention, therefore, more towards the old ale and the
steak-and-kidney pie and less towards his companions. The
temperature at his end of the table cooled; the ladies drooped
disappointedly. At the other end, among the cricketers, a
definite thaw set in, and one of the players thought for a
moment of addressing a comparatively civil remark to the
mountebank who had so let down the prestige of the Old
School by becoming a film actor.

After luncheon the game was resumed, but knitting,
sewing, novels, even the charms of gentle sleep, were all
abandoned, and every feminine eye was fixed upon the swift
and graceful extra-cover-point.

The County players settled down again and the score had
risen to 180, when Vernon held a brief consultation with his
wicket-keeper, then shrugged his shoulders like a man who
has to make the best of a bad job, and went up to Hugo.

'D'you bowl at all?' he asked curtly.

'I think so,' replied Hugo.

Vernon looked at him sourly as if to say, 'More monkey-
tricks, eh?' and then said, 'Next over. That end.'

And so began, with those four brief words, the final chain
of events, inexorable, inescapable, foredoomed, that was to
bring Hugo to ultimate disaster.

Poor Hugo. He did not know it. At that moment the
world was perfection for him. There was no hint that Nemesis might be at work. Only a voice kept repeating somewhere inside him, 'You're going to bowl in a real cricket-
match, you're going to bowl in a real cricket-match.'

Treading on air, Hugo walked to the far wicket at the end of the over and rolled up his sleeve and took the ball. 'Right hand over the wicket,' he told the umpire, and then he paced out his run. 'Eight yards, never more,' Uncle Eustace had said so often.

Then he began to place his field.

The spectators watched in breathless silence.

Hugo bowled with a sharp off-break, and his bowling was the fastest ever seen on that ground or any other ground in the county of Suffolk. In four overs he clean-bowled nine batsmen, broke two stumps, hit the tenth batsman on the body and broke a rib, and broke three fingers on the wicket-keeper's left hand, and severely bruised both hands of the deputy wicket-keeper.

In an awed silence the fielding team returned to the pavilion. The total was 186. Hugo had taken nine wickets for four runs. The four runs were a snick through the slips that reached the boundary in a flash.

Mr Vernon, by this time distinctly more respectful in manner, approached Hugo and asked him if he would bat first for the home team.

'I'm afraid,' replied Hugo, 'that I am not a good batsman. I can only keep my bat straight,' and then he added automatically, 'on and off the field.'

Mr Vernon looked at him suspiciously, as if he was afraid his Old Etonian leg was being pulled, but Hugo's air of unconscious simplicity was most disarming.

'Very well,' he said. 'I'll put you in sixth. You'll find pads and gloves in the pavilion.'

Hugo batted sixth and kept his bat so rigidly straight that his defence was quite impregnable, and he retired undefeated at the end of the innings, having compiled seven runs in an hour and twenty minutes.

While the teams were packing their belongings into cricket-bags, and drinking beer, and talking in little groups, and carrying trays of cocktails to the ladies, Hugo perceived an animated discussion in progress between the two Middle-

sex batsmen who had batted first for the visiting team, and
an older man in a Zingari blazer. All three were talking in
vehement undertones, though once one of the county players
raised his right hand as high as possible above his head and
exclaimed loudly, 'Marvellous, I tell you.'

A few minutes later the man in the Zingari blazer came
up to Hugo and said, 'Would you care to come up to London
tomorrow, Seeley, and have a net at Lord's?'

'At Lord's!' exclaimed Hugo with a thrill of excitement.
'Do you really mean that?'

'Of course I do,' replied the other, 'and perhaps you'll be
my guest at luncheon in the Pavilion afterwards. Shall we
say half-past eleven? Good.'

Hugo resisted with some reluctance and a great deal of
difficulty the combined pressure of the ladies to stay to
dinner and spend the night in the red-brick, battlemented,
moated manor-house that here and there appeared through
the trees. He wanted to spend a quiet and abstemious evening, and go to bed early, so as to be as fit and as fresh as
possible next morning for his net on the famous ground
which he had heard Uncle Eustace describe so often as literally the Mecca of the cricket world. He found it easier to
resist Mr Vernon's invitation to stop and take pot-luck at
supper. The moment he had begun to indicate that his
answer was likely to be in the negative, Mr Vernon had
brightened perceptibly and had interrupted, 'Got to rush off,
have you? Well, many thanks for turning out. So long.'

The famous film star bowed to each of the saddened ladies,
and strolled home across the meadows through the scented
English evening, his feet upon Suffolk buttercups and his
head among the eternal stars.

There was no match at Lord's on that June morning, and
Hugo gazed in silence at the empty arena. How well he
knew it, although he had never seen it. There was the Mound
Stand over which Victor Trumper had hit Schofield Haigh
in the first over of a Test Match. There was the wicket on

which Spofforth, the Demon, had routed the strength of England in a single day with his tremendous bowling. There was the Pavilion over which only Albert Trott had ever hit a cricket-ball. There were the steps down which the mighty figure of the Doctor had walked year after year, on his way to smite, year after year, the bowling of the Players of England.

Who shall resist all resistless Graces?

as the poet asked in despair. To Hugo the ground was full of ghosts—Thomas Lord who made it, and those who came after and adorned it, Alfred Mynn and Fuller Pilch, Silver Billy Beldham and Felix and Squire Osbaldestone and Lambert and that fiery parson the Lord Frederick Beauclerk, and Shaw and Shrewsbury, and Spofforth, that grim Australian, and Trumble, and Kumar Shri Ranjitsinjhi, and Tom Hayward, and Tom Richardson, and the immortal band of Yorkshiremen. All these were household names to Hugo, freshly remembered. Tears came into his eyes, as he looked at the silhouetted figure of old, long-bearded Father Time on the top of the new stand, taking the bails inexorably off the stumps, and instinctively he found himself murmuring:

For the field is full of shades as I near the shadowy coast,
And a ghostly batsman plays to the bowling of a ghost,
And I look through my tears on a soundless-clapping host
　　As the run-stealers flicker to and fro,
　　　　To and fro:—
Oh my Hornby and my Barlow long ago.

Then he gave his eyes a furtive dab with his handkerchief and went round to the Pavilion, handed in his name, and was taken off at once to a changing-room.

The cricketing-nursery at the east end of Lord's was humming with its usual activity. Young professionals were bowling away at middle-aged members of the M.C.C. and the air was filled with the sounds of bat on ball, and the sounds

of ball upon stumps, and the gently laudatory cries of 'Well
played, sir.' But Hugo was guided past these nets to a mysterious enclosure of green canvas, and then the 'door' was
carefully closed. Inside the enclosure there was another net,
with stumps ready and creases marked out; a young man in
flannels, pads, and gloves, was leaning upon a bat; and
behind the net were standing three men, shining in morning-
coats and silk hats and gardenia buttonholes. As Hugo came
in, one of the three hooked an imaginary ball off his left ear
with an exquisitely rolled silken umbrella and the other two
watched gravely. Near this vision of masculine sartorialism
were two other men, in ordinary suits and soft hats and very
solid, well-made boots. Both were of medium height and
both were about fifty years of age. One was thin, with a
thin face and a long, bird-like nose, while the other's face
was round and red and rustic. They stood about two yards
from the men in the silk hats, and the distance, neither too
far nor too near, seemed to convey a certain deference to
superiors, and at the same time a readiness to join in the
conversation at any moment as independent equals.

Hugo was introduced to the prospective batsman. He
could not catch his name, but he understood that he came
from Gloucestershire. A handful of new cricket-balls was
produced, and Hugo measured out his run. For half an hour
he pounded away at the young man and was surprised, and
indeed rather piqued, at his inability to bowl him out more
than twice. On the other hand, the young man treated the
terrific onslaught with the utmost deference, dodging the
high-kickers, and leaping with extraordinary agility out of
the way of the lightning expresses that pitched just outside
the leg-stump. The five men behind the net watched every
ball intently. At the end of the half-hour there was a pause,
and Hugo heard one of the silk-hatted gentlemen call out to
the red-faced man, 'Like a knock, Wilfred?'

'Ah'm not such a fooil, Sir Francis, Try Jack here,' said
the red-faced man in a north country accent and they all
laughed, and the thin, bird-like man shook his head cheer-

fully. 'Not me, sir. I survived Gregory and Macdonald and I'm not going to risk my life now.'

The five men then put their heads together and talked earnestly for a minute. Hugo sat down on the grass for a rest, although his training was so good that he felt as if he could go on bowling for hours. The batsman was summoned to the secret palaver and there was much nodding of heads.

Finally one of the immaculate gentlemen left the group and came across to Hugo. 'I must introduce myself, Mr Seeley,' he said, as Hugo scrambled to his feet. 'My name is Sir Francis Wilson, and I am the Chairman of the M.C.C.'s Selection Committee. Those two gentlemen are my colleagues, and the other two are our professional advisers. I don't think they need any introduction,' he added with a smile. Hugo, who knew neither the names nor the faces of the two professionals, nor any reason why they did not need any introduction, thought it best to say nothing. 'We have unanimously decided,' went on Sir Francis, 'to invite you to play in the second Test Match against Borealia, which begins next Friday on this ground.'

Hugo was staggered. The scene went dim. His voice vanished somewhere down into his chest, and he had no subsequent recollection of any circumstance whatsoever until he found himself, returned to ordinary clothes, on the top of a bus in the vicinity of the Marble Arch, staring down at posters of evening newspapers, which trumpeted out the tidings 'Unparalleled Test Sensation', and 'Mystery Test Cricketer'.

The Great Day dawned misty but warm. There was dew on the grass at Lord's and the famous sparrows darted impertinently from one fairy mesh to another in search of incautious worms and crumbs left over from the match of two days before.

At 6 a.m. the queue of spectators with their three-legged stools stretched as far as St John's Wood Road Station, and by 10 a.m. twenty thousand people were sitting on newspapers in the street. At half-past ten the gates were opened; at a quarter to twelve the Prime Minister took his seat in the Pavilion; and at one minute to twelve His Majesty the King, His Royal Highness the Prince of Wales, Gold Stick-in-Waiting, the Gentleman-Usher of the Black Rod, seven Grooms of the Bed-Chamber, the ex-Sub-Dean of the Chapel Royal and Deputy Clerk of the Closet, and the Master of the Horse, arrived and were greeted with the tempestuous cheering of forty thousand loyal citizens of the far-flung Empire.

At twelve o'clock precisely, in a warm sunshine and under a blue, windless sky, the English captain led his team amid another tremendous burst of cheering down the steps of the Pavilion and out to the wicket. The eleven men gazed wisely and intently at the pitch and one or two of them threw a ball idly from hand to hand. Then a third roar—much of it resounding from the section of the stands which had been allotted to the Borealian spectators—with a curiously pitched accent, heralded the appearance of Borealia's opening batsmen.

One of the umpires handed a new ball to the English captain, who handed it in turn to Hugo.

'You start, Seeley,' he said laconically. 'Pavilion end. What slips do you want?'

'One,' replied Hugo firmly, 'and five short-legs.'

The English captain looked at him queerly. 'They told me you were a fast bowler,' he said.

'I mix 'em,' replied Hugo, pinning all his faith in Uncle Eustace. For what was it Uncle Eustace had said so often? 'When in doubt put five men on the leg-side and bowl at the leg-stump.' That was the ticket.

As the batsmen were walking out, a great silence fell upon the ground, that silence which Elia says is multiplied and made more intense by numbers. But when the first two men took up their stations almost at the batsman's elbow, there came a muttering in the Borealian corner of the vast crowd, like the rolling of far-off thunder over downland, rising for a moment to a menacing growl, and dying away behind the slopes of grass, and rising again in a sullen boom. As the third short-leg and then the fourth and then the fifth took post, 'You heard as if an army muttered; and the muttering grew to a grumbling; and the grumbling grew to a mighty rumbling,' and then the noise died away into a sultry, tense, hot, silence.

There was not a sound. The stillness of forty thousand beings lay across the arena. But there was a deadly menace in the air.

The Borealian batsman was ready. The wicket-keeper, the slip-fieldsman, and short-legs crouched, and the other fieldsmen began to walk towards the wicket. Hugo ran up to the wicket and delivered a levin-bolt at the leg stump. The ball jumped sharply and hit the batsman in the ribs. Instantly there was a roar of fury from the Borealian corner. It was a terrible sound, like a thousand hungry lions, or revolutionaries baying for the blood of aristocrats.

Hugo apologised to the Borealian and walked back. Again he ran up the wicket, gracefully and yet compact with power and energy, and down flashed the ball again upon the leg-stump. The Borealian tried to defend himself against the bolt, and was easily caught by one of the short-legs, and then the Borealian spectators, ten thousand strong, let loose a terrific yell and surged over the ropes like the bursting of a gigantic sluice, and rushed towards Hugo. In a moment the air was full of dust, and queer-shaped felt hats with very large brims, and raucous cries in the strange accent that seemed to be partly American and partly Cockney, and whirling boomerangs, and oranges, and flagon-shaped bottles, and horrid black bottle-tops with a screw thread. Here and there pet kangaroos were leaping about the ground like maniacal acrobats. Wallabies howled at the Pavilion. Opossums, escaping from their masters, danced wild dances in front of the sight-screen at the nursery-end, while omnivorous bandicoots lived up to their epithet by devouring impartially hats, paper-bags, oranges, and boomerangs.

A flying squirrel perched on the score-board, and a root-eating wombat, balancing itself upon the railings of the Pavilion, wailed its mournful song into the unwilling ear of the oldest member of the M.C.C., who was jammed into a corner beside the rails and was unable to move.

It was, in short, a stirring sight, a wholly unprecedented sight, and, as seen by Hugo and his colleagues, a not altogether pleasing sight. However, its lack of pleasing effect was compensated for by its very short duration, for, after a single appalled moment, the English team took to its heels and bolted for the protection of the Mound Stand, leaving the playing-field, the pride and joy of old Thomas Lord, in the undisputed possession of the fauna, if not perhaps of the flora, of the great Dominion of Borealia.

Once lost in the dense masses of spectators which clung in festoons to every seat, railing, and square foot of space, on the Mound, the team began to feel a little safer, and after a short time they were smuggled down to one of the batmakers' shops below. In the meanwhile pandemonium was raging on the ground.

The Borealians, stern, lean men with brown, clear-cut faces and a not especially developed cranial development, were soon torn between two conflicting emotions. And one idea at a time is difficult enough for a simple son of backwoods and bushrangers and sheep-dips to assimilate; the simultaneous impingement of two notions upon those classic brows was the devil and all. The cruel dilemma played Old Harry with the usually self-reliant Borealian power to make a decision. These ten thousand strong men, and to a somewhat lesser extent the kangaroos and bandicoots and other pets, were thirsting for the blood of the iniquitous ruffian, the dastardly scoundrel, the monstrous villain, who had revived the 'body-line' controversy by placing five men close in on the leg-side and bowling like lightning at the batsman. At the same time these ten thousand simple souls were longing to sing *Land of Hope and Glory* in front of the Pavilion, as a gesture of Imperial solidarity and goodwill. They paused

irresolutely in the middle of the ground. The bottles stopped
flying through the air and came to rest on the turf, displaying
their gay labels in the sun, Château Lafitte Paramatta,
Château Yquem Wagga-Wagga, Coolgardie Beaujolais, and
Bendigo Beaune, and many another delicious product of the
Southern Vineyard. The kangaroos stopped bounding. The
omnivorous bandicoots looked up from their meal of walking-sticks and early editions of the evening newspapers, and
even the flying squirrel stopped tearing pieces out of the
score-board and throwing them at the scorers.

A strange hush fell over the ground, broken only by the
dreary wail of the root-eating wombat into the oldest member's ear. So melancholy was the dirge, so heartrending the
long cadences, that it seemed to be an even-money chance
whether the wombat died of a broken heart before the oldest
member had a fit of apoplexy.

Then the tension was broken by a loud shout from the
balcony of the Pavilion. It was the Secretary of State for the
Dominions, megaphone in hand, a gay, gallant figure in
morning-coat, striped trousers, grey top-hat, orchid button-
hole, and white spats. The crowd of Borealians instinctively
crowded towards the Pavilion to hear what the ever-popular
Cabinet Minister had got to say.

He lifted the megaphone and shouted, in the voice that
had dominated a thousand meetings, "Ere, why not start the
blinking game again? we'll 'oof that blighter hout, and start
fair. Wotchersay?'

A roar of applause made it clear what the Borealians
wanted to say.

'Then get to it, me boys,' roared the Cabinet Minister,
and the situation was saved. The Borealians as one man
struck up *Land of Hope and Glory* and sang it right through,
every verse of it, completely drowning, and thus profoundly
discouraging, the melancholious wombat, and then strode,
with that famous long, loose stride of the backwoods, to
their seats, whistled in their pets, and prepared to enjoy the
game once more.

The English team re-emerged, with the twelfth man substituted for Hugo, and the Second Test Match began for the second time.

In a small room in the Pavilion of the Marylebone Cricket Club, a grim scene was being played. The room faced north, so that no sunshine brightened the dark sombreness that shadowed the faces of the actors. Out of the window nothing could be seen except the fantastic excrescences of grimy red and still grimier white which are called, in St John's Wood, blocks of residential flats. In that dreary vista there was no suggestion either of a glade of trees or of the holy apostle. Everything was drab.

Hugo, bewildered, harassed, dejected, sat all crumpled up on a hard wooden chair. The President of the M.C.C. stood leaning moodily upon a small desk. He was in a scowling rage, and was tapping the floor impatiently with his foot. He obviously was anxious to get back to his seat and watch the game. Some sort of permanent official of the club was hovering behind him. Two enormous policemen stood one on each side of the door, in identical attitudes of corpulent alertness. Opposite Hugo sat the Secretary of State for Dominion Affairs, talking, talking, talking. Hugo hardly listened. He could not understand what had happened. Apparently he had committed some hideous and unforgivable crime in getting that Borealian batsman caught like that. But what crime could it be? He had spent hours before the Test Match began in studying the 1934 Laws of Cricket to see if they differed in any way from the Laws in Uncle Eustace's time, and nowhere had he discovered that it was a crime to get a batsman out like that. And now that he came to think of it, during the second or two that had elapsed between the dismissal of the batsman and the irruption of raging, torrential Borealia upon the playing-field, there had been time for the umpire to remonstrate with him if he had been playing unfairly. But the umpire had said nothing. The umpire clearly saw nothing wrong, and did not the Laws of

Cricket say, in Law 34, 'The Umpires are the sole judges of fair or unfair play'? And if that was so, why did he have to fly for his life from the ground, and then, what was almost worse, have to listen to this portentously pompous statesman droning away interminably? And why policemen at the door?

What was the old fool saying? "Ow do you expect me to land a rebate on the tariff on whipple-sprockets that Birmingham is 'owling for,' he was shouting, as he hammered the palm of one hand with the fist of the other, 'if you play old blasted 'Arry like this with Borealian Suscip-suscibbi—well, you knows what I mean.'

Hugo had not the faintest idea what he meant.

'And there's the contract for the rotary bevil-flanges for the new power station,' went on the politician vehemently. 'Coventry 'ad as good as got the job, and now I'll 'ave to slog like 'ell to save it from going to Krupps. And then there's the new suspension bridge. Oh my God!'—his voice rose to a wail—'I'd forgotten the new suspension bridge. Ninety thousand tons of Durham steel.' He wrung his hands in despair.

'What on earth,' asked Hugo wearily, 'has a game of cricket got to do with ninety thousand tons of Durham steel?'

'Young man,' said the Cabinet Minister with a dreadful emphasis upon every word, 'that is not a game of cricket. It is a link of Empire. It brings together the mother and daughter countries in a way that nothing else can. Do you realise that if I had not been on that balcony just now, and had not exerted the full force of my personality, there would by now, already, be a very definite chance of the secession of Borealia from our far-flung Empire and her absorption into the Empire of Japan?'

'Good heavens!' The President of the M.C.C. started out of his fidgety apathy. 'You don't mean that, sir?'

'I do, sir,' was the stern reply.

The President seemed knocked all of a heap. 'No more Test Matches,' he muttered over and over again.

The Dominions Secretary turned his attention to Hugo again. 'They tell me you're an 'Ollywood film star.'

'No, I'm not,' said Hugo sulkily. 'At least, I am.'

'You'd better make up your mind,' said the Minister grimly. 'Because you're going to be deported to the United States tomorrow.'

'For getting a Borealian batsman caught at short-leg?' demanded Hugo indignantly.

'For hendangering hour himperial 'armonies, and for 'ampering hour hexporting hindustries,' came the slow, magniloquent, overwhelming reply.

Hugo, more convinced than ever that he was dealing solely and exclusively with maniacs, from highest to lowest, shrank back in his chair from this terrible indictment, and thought it best to say nothing.

The interview was over. The Minister, the President, and the permanent functionary filed out, and two policemen escorted Hugo to the dressing-room, and thence to a taxi, and thence to his hotel. They had orders, they explained, not to leave him until he was safely on board the American liner. As the trio left Lord's, they heard the loud, raucous, exultant cries of the Borealian supporters, as their champions smote the slow and medium-paced deliveries of the remaining English bowlers all over the field.

The Unrecorded Test Match

by LORD DUNSANY

The eccentric Irish nobleman and writer, Lord Dunsany — once called 'the worst dressed man in Ireland' — would be worth having in any team for his impact on opponents. Alec Waugh, who saw him play in a curious charity match between Actors and Actresses using a soft ball, wrote a few years ago, 'Dunsany arrived in an impressive blazer, carrying a heavy and well-worn leather cricket bat, to treat the proceedings with an unsmiling solemnity as though he were taking part in a real match.'

Dunsany, in fact, took his love of cricket to extraordinary lengths — he not only raised a team in Ireland to play either at home or in England, but also laid out his own wicket in the grounds of his ancestral home in County Meath. He was a left-handed batsman and a good pace bowler with a reputation for whipping in full tosses at rural batsmen who might be intimidated by his speed or his towering 6 feet 2 inch frame. Dunsany was also notorious for his practical jokes — and apparently carried a clockwork duck in his cricket bag which he would wind up and send waddling out to meet any batsman unfortunate enough not to have scored!

In the course of a busy working life as a novelist, dramatist and poet, he produced over sixty books, a considerable number of these being humorous. He also created an unforgettable storyteller — Jorkens — who, for the price of a whisky or two, entertains fellow members of a billiards club with the most outrageous stories. Several of these tall tales are, not surprisingly, about cricket, and I commend 'The Unrecorded Test Match' as being one of the best.

T<small>ALK</small> was general at the Billiards Club, one day over our lunch, I forget what it was all about, but somebody must have mentioned the Devil, for I heard Jorkens' voice raised suddenly over the rest, saying, 'Keep away from the Devil. Have nothing to do with him.'

'Oh?' said Terbut, who was one of us at our long table. 'I thought he was rather a friend of yours.'

'Not one that can be trusted,' said Jorkens.

'You don't trust him, then?' said Terbut.

'Certainly not,' said Jorkens. 'Nor will you any more, after you've heard what I have to tell you about him.'

'And what is that?' asked Terbut. And so we got this story.

'It's what a man told me only the other day,' said Jorkens, 'a friend of mine to whom I had given a drink. He told me the story just after the drink. They do say *In vino veritas*, you know.'

'We shouldn't doubt any friend of yours,' said Terbut.

'No,' said Jorkens. 'Well, what happened, he told me, was this: he was young, and one night he went to the wrong kind of house. He admits that. And there he met the Devil. He met him just inside the door in evening dress; white waistcoat, neat white tie; and a long black cloak all open in front and hanging down from his shoulders. He was perfectly dressed. For a moment my friend was taken aback, and muttered some apology.

' "Not at all," said the Devil. "After you."

'And he slightly bowed, and stood aside and waved to my friend to come in. And in Porlick went: that was his name. He said there was such a charm in the Devil's manner that you could hardly help doing as he said. And as he walked past him the Devil asked, "Is there anything I can do for you?"

'He hardly liked to refuse the offer. And at first he thought of asking for something he would not tell me. And then all at once, as he stood in front of the Devil, his thoughts went right away from that dingy house, and away from all he had thought at first of asking, and visited green fields of the open country. And without any more consideration he blurted out, "You can. Would you be so kind as to give me the power to take twenty wickets in that number of balls."

' "Certainly," said the Devil.

' "And the price?" said Porlick. For he had made up his mind not to let the Devil have his soul. And he thinks the Devil must have seen that in his face; for all he asked in exchange was one of Porlick's virtues. He said that the Devil waved a finger in the air then; he thinks twenty times. And then he vanished.

'Porlick had no doubt that the spell, or whatever it was, would work. You see, he had seen the Devil. And what is more, he trusted him. I suppose that to win people's trust is the first thing the Devil is able to do. Even bad men in business can do that. Indeed, it is the basis of all their business. For all that, he wanted to be quite sure; and he decided to allocate one of his magic balls to finding out. What he decided to do was to get the best batsman that he could find and bowl one ball to him, and see if it worked. Or not the best batsman that he could find, because he would hardly allow an unknown young man to make the experiment on him; but the best batsman who could be persuaded to stand up to one ball from Porlick. This experimental ball would of course upset the idea that had prompted Porlick's impulsive request, uttered hurriedly and without time for consideration, which was to get all the wickets in a big match for no runs. He could probably have asked for something that would have been far more useful to him, but we don't all take advantage of our opportunities, even when we have time to think them over. Forgive my moralising.

'Well, Porlick haunted cricket grounds after that, anywhere in the county to which buses could carry him, whenever a match was being played. He would watch the men batting and choose a good batsman, but it was not so easy to go up to him afterwards and be allowed to bowl a ball to him at the nets. The difficulty was that such a request required an introduction from some other cricketer, and any cricketer who knew young Porlick knew he could hardly bowl at all. Not many did know him, and the ones that didn't of course would not help him, while those who knew how he bowled would be even less inclined to do so. At last he got an introduction without saying what he wanted to do, and talked with a very good batsman, at first about other things, and just before the cricketer got tired of him and before he shook him off, he made his request. The man that had introduced him had luckily gone, so that he was able to represent himself as a young bowler who had got many wickets and was hoping to get a place one day on some better team than any that came his way, that might want a good bowler. And the man he was talking to was a kindly fellow and liked to encourage the young, and put on his pads and went to the nets with young Porlick. And Porlick scattered his stumps. That batsman was a man who had sometimes played for the county, and he was surprised and interested and asked Porlick to go on bowling. But Porlick just walked away. He couldn't think of any excuse, so he just left. He had satisfied himself that the spell worked, or, as he put it, that the Devil was playing fair, which is just what that sort of people always seem to be doing, until it is too late. He knew he could never bowl at that pace, or pitch a ball as that ball had been pitched; and he had nineteen balls left, and the world, as it seemed, before him. County cricket was of no interest to him, and he went straight away from that cricket field, and next day he was in London, where the Australians were. A totally unknown boy of about nineteen was determined to play in a Test Match against the Australians. And, after all, why not? He had the greatest power in the world to back him. Yes, I am afraid it is the greatest power. If not, it's a near thing. But at any rate it was enough to win a cricket match. Porlick, with little money and mighty dreams, found lodgings in London, and devoted all his time to getting an introduction to the captain of the English XI, which he like everyone else called the England side; and sometimes he used to talk of the England side captain. And at last he found a man who knew one of the team. That was something, indeed much; but at first it led no further. This acquaintance that Porlick made would not introduce a young man unknown for everything, and especially for cricket, to a member of the English XI. Porlick spoke glowingly of his own prowess as a bowler, but that was not enough, and he soon saw that he would have to give up one of the magic balls as a demonstration. He persuaded his new acquaintance to lunch with him at an hotel. How he managed that I don't know, and it used up about half of his money. And over that lunch he persuaded the man, who was a cricketer, that if he could bowl him out, the first ball, he would go with him to Lord's on the opening day against the Australians and introduce Porlick to his friend, who was playing for England. Well, this acquaintance that Porlick made was a member of the M.C.C., a man called Trennle.

'And they decided between them that the simple way of doing it would be to go to Lord's early on the first day of the match and for Porlick to bowl his ball at the nets, and that, if he succeeded in bowling Trennle, he should go along and be introduced to Hathway, who would be playing for England. And all that happened. Porlick did bowl out Trennle, much to his surprise, and Trennle kept his word; he kept it with the fervour of a man who has lost a bet and is honourably determined to pay. He ran down Hathway, went up to him and accosted him, and then introduced Porlick as a promising young cricketer. Hathway was not much interested; but there are things, such as Niagara and the Himalayas, that are too vast for us to ignore, and the audacity of Porlick's remark to him was one of them. For when he saw that Hathway was taking no particular notice of him he said, "I could bowl out the Australians in under two overs."

'And behind his words, in a way that I can't explain, was that strength that seems to be given to any remark by Truth. Some echo from Truth's own voice perhaps blended with sheer amazement in Hathway's mind, and at least made him notice Porlick. Trennle tried to explain away the boy's outburst, but he and Hathway remained quite silent. And then Porlick said, "If the captain would let me bowl a ball to him he would see."

' "I am afraid he wouldn't have time for that," said Hathway.

' "No, no, no," said Trennle.

'And Porlick seemed to be getting no further. He saw then that, to get anywhere, more of those magic balls would have to be thrown away than he thought. Hathway was turning away from him, when he said, "Won't you see if I can do what I say? Won't you let me bowl one ball to you?"

'Hathway stopped in his turn, and a thought must have gone through his mind; for he said to his friend Trennle, "After all, there are infant prodigies."

' "Oh, no, I don't think so," said Trennle, or something like that.

'And Hathway stood quite still. I think they rather wanted a bowler. But this looked like a mad dream.

' "Only one ball," said Porlick.

' "Oh, very well," said Hathway, perhaps feeling that one ball at the nets would be less trouble than further pursuit of the thoughts that were now puzzling him.

'They went, all three, to the nets.

' "You haven't got any spikes," said Hathway.

' "That won't matter," said Porlick.

'Nor did it matter. Nothing mattered, with that power that rules the world, or is a very close runner-up, to back him.

' "Will you introduce me to the captain if I bowl you out?" said Porlick.

' "Oh, yes," said Hathway nonchalantly.

'And Porlick bowled, and Hathway's wickets were scattered.

' "Wait a minute," said Hathway. "Do you mind doing that again? I don't think I can quite have been ready."

'It was easily said, and lightly said. Matches aren't played at the nets; there are no runs there; nothing is concerned. Or so thought Hathway. To Porlick it was an almost overwhelming blow. With three balls gone already, and more required before he could hope to play for England, there was no longer any chance of his bowling out the Australians for no runs, as he had hoped. He would have to make his name on one innings only. Good enough for him. He determined to be as economical as he could with the Devil's magic. But a fourth ball must go. So he walked sadly back as Hathway replaced the bails, and he bowled again, and with the same result.

' "Odd," said Hathway. "Well, I will introduce you to the captain."

'Porlick thanked him profusely.

' "I can't say that he'll go to the nets with you. But I'll tell him you're too good for me."

'Porlick thanked him again.

' "I expect the light's a bit bad there," said Trennle.

' "Oh, no," said Hathway, for he was a sportsman.

'They walked to the pavilion, Hathway looking a little puzzled. There was a quarter of an hour to go before the start of the match. Hathway had been able to bring the young man to the nets, but even he, though playing for England that day, could not bring him into the pavilion. So he left him at the gate and went in with Trennle, and brought the captain out to him. And this was a very great deal for him to have done for the young fellow; but Porlick was still a long way from playing against the Australians. Perhaps a vast ambition is best after all, but it has obstacles in its way, that little ambitions know nothing about. What do you think?'

'Well, I don't know,' said someone, and began to express an opinion. And others came in with other opinions, and the conversation was sliding fast away from that devilish magic. It was I that brought it back.

When Jorkens returned to his story he said, 'The captain seems to have been quite polite to young Porlick, but he was obviously preoccupied, as who wouldn't be on such an occasion? Hathway told him that Porlick had just bowled him out.

' "Twice," said Porlick.

' "Well, I wasn't quite ready the first time," Hathway said. "But it was a well-pitched ball.'

'Thus he brushed away one of the most difficult balls to play that had ever been bowled in England.

' "You want me to see you bowl?" he said, always on the look out for young talent, though Porlick didn't look at all the boy to possess it.

' "Oh, yes please, sir," said Porlick

' "I am afraid I have no time now," said the captain.

'Those blessed words rang in young Porlick's ears like bells from a promised land, faint and far-off indeed, and yet full of hope; and he felt that his chance was going to be given him. You may think that I speak rather ecstatically, indeed that I exaggerate. But I can assure you, having spoken with Porlick and having heard his whole story, that nothing that I can say can make you appreciate what his ambition meant to him, which was nothing less than what I have told you, to play against the Australians and bowl them all out with ten balls. He still had sixteen left.

'The luncheon interval came, and the captain remembered Porlick. What I imagine happened, from something that Porlick said, though I don't think he realised it himself, was that the captain, who had been fielding all the morning, had heard some talk of a new Australian bowler, and rather wanted a little practice to get his eye in and probably welcomed something as young and new as Porlick, looking perhaps to find in him that touch of mystery with which people were crediting the Australian. I don't say that rumour in cricket can make a ball swerve another inch, but it will sometimes add to a bowler a fear that can be as unsettling to a batsman, before he has got his eye in, as a swerve of half a yard; and I think that the English captain that morning wanted to see some bowling that was new and a little strange before he went in to bat. That is only my conjecture. It may have been mere kindness. But whatever the reason, he took young Porlick over to the nets, and allowed him to bowl to him. Well, of course, there was no standing up to the Devil, and the captain's bails and stumps went the way of all who had batted against those spells.

' "H'm," said the captain. "Will you send down another?"

'He didn't know he was asking for Porlick's heart's-blood. Or that's what the young fellow called it when he told the tale to me.

' "It will be just the same," said Porlick. But the captain naturally wanted to see for himself. And Porlick bowled again; of course with the same result.

' "I don't think I can be in very good form today," said the captain. "Would you mind bowling again?"

'Despair gripped Porlick by the throat, so that at first he could not speak.

' "If you will play me in the next Test Match I will," he said.

'Such words, if ever uttered before, the captain had never heard, and even what he had just seen did nothing to diminish the shock of them, and he stood speechless. A young man was bargaining with him with the audacity of Lot trying to save Gomorrah.

' "I don't think we could do that," he said at last.

' "After all," said Porlick, "it will be the hat-trick."

' "I don't think you will do it again," said the captain.

' "But if I do do it again?" said Porlick

' "I might think about it then," said the captain.

' "And I guarantee," said Porlick, "to get three hat-tricks against them when you play me."

' "What?" said the captain. And Porlick repeated it.

' "Well, send down another and let me see," said the captain.

' "Will you play me in the Test if I do?" asked Porlick.

'Again that audacious demand. There had been nothing like it since Lot.

'Never before having had such an unblushing request made to him the captain hardly knew what to say, and rashly decided to end this difficult conversation in a way he felt perfectly safe. Hathway and Trennle, I should have told you, were watching, and they both heard his words. "All right," he said. "If you bowl me this time." And as he said it he determined to end the whole business by going on the defensive as he would have done if he had to save the game by surviving the last ball of a match. I don't quite know how. But when he was on the defensive, not in search of any runs, but only determined to keep up his wicket, there was probably no one in Australia or England who was able to get him out. Of course it was very seldom he played that way, because he wanted runs. But, when he did, he was invincible. No *man* in Australia or England, I should have said, but against the Devil it was of course a different matter. He stood with his bat perfectly steady, but the ball came in

round it and got his middle stump, a very fast ball that
scattered everything.

' "Thank you, sir," said Porlick, and walked away to
avoid any argument, and the captain and Hathway and
Trennle were left together. What they arranged I don't
know, for Porlick never heard them. But he had bowled out
all three of them, and six times with six balls. Porlick gathered that at least one of the men had been prepared to say
that the captain had not really given a definite promise, and
that the captain had said, "We might try him." What the
English needs for a new bowler may have been at that time
I do not know, nor any of the influences at work. And of
course none of them had ever seen Porlick bat or field. In
this he was lucky, for though he did not look the sort of
boy that was either able to field or to make a good bat, no
amount of mere appearances could have shown those three
cricketers how bad he really was in the field or at the wicket.
Of course Porlick knew that, at any rate in the first innings,
he need only field for one over, if only they put him on
first. But they could not know that. Porlick went back to
his lodgings and wrote to the captain, merely reminding him
of his promise and asking the date of the next Test Match.
Then with what was left of his money he bought some
adequate flannels and waited. And the odd thing was that,
whatever influences worked, and however they worked, he
got a letter from the selection committee that week, saying
that he had been selected to play against the Australians in
a match, at a date that was given, in the North Country.
Well, the days went by and the day of the match arrived. I
say that the days went by, however obvious it may be to all
of you, because it really seemed to Porlick that the day
would never come. But it did. They played on the high
ground above Hawnby, I think he said. But wherever they
played, there was Porlick, wearing the English cap. However
incompetent he was with a bat he seems to have had a certain
ability with his tongue, and with his usual audacity and with
a certain amount of skill in stating his case he approached

the captain as soon as he lost the toss and urged that he should put him on first to bowl. "You've backed me," said Porlick, "and, if you've made a mistake, the sooner you find it out the better. I solemnly promise you that, if I do not start with a hat-trick, I will strain my ankle or something and retire. Whereas, if I can do what I promised, the sooner we get those Australians out the better." Before such impudence the captain was almost dumb, being totally unaccustomed to it. And Porlick went on, "To tell you the truth," and it was the absolute truth, "I am a very poor fielder. But let me bowl, and you'll see."

'And he did see. And many thousand people saw. For he put Porlick on to bowl from the moor end, the first over of the match, as he had asked. For a minute, Porlick told me, he felt some trace of nervousness, but as he walked back from the wicket with the ball in his hand and realised the enormous power that was behind him, all nervousness went away, and he ran casually up to the bowling-crease and flung the ball without even troubling to think where it was going to pitch. Why should he? He knew nothing that he could do would send down a ball that would be worthy to be bowled at a Test Match, or in any decent cricket. So why bother? In this careless mood he bowled. And the ball was what one might have expected from inexperience and carelessness. But not what Porlick expected. It was not one of those fast ones that he had bowled at the nets: it flew up out of his hand high into the air, going slowly up and up, and then began to drop towards the wicket. The Australian batsman looked at it in amazement. The crowd started to laugh. And then the Australian, seeing that it was going to drop somewhere near the wicket, hit at it with his bat, as one might hit at a tiresome bluebottle, downwards towards the off, and it hit the toe of the boot of first slip, who was standing close in, and bounced up and fell into the hands of second slip. The umpire, of course, gave it out. But most of the crowd supposed that the ball had hit the ground, and the Australian part of it turned from their laughter to a sudden roar of anger, as they saw their best batsman walking away. Porlick felt a fool, and most of the rest of the team gave a rather pitying glance at him. But the captain walked straight up to the young man, and told him not to be discouraged. A new ball was sometimes slippery, he said untruthfully, and a thing like that might happen to anybody.

' "Don't think about it," he said. "Never mind the crowd. And now bowl as you bowled to me."

'The captain walked back to his place as another Australian came in, and Porlick went back to the point from which he started his run, determined to add all his own energy to the mighty power of the Devil, not that that addition could mean much. But the combined effort of the Devil and Porlick seemed unable this time to send the ball the whole length of the pitch: it flew a few yards from his hand, dropped short of the middle of the pitch and trickled slowly up it, while the whole crowd, English and Australian, laughed. The batsman, when it reached him, seeing that it had practically stopped, kicked it contemptuously back to Porlick. Porlick appealed. The ball was dead straight, and the umpire, not being able to judge its exact pace at that distance, and so not realising that it would never have reached the wicket at all, gave it out. Porlick told me that he had not wished to appeal, but that some great inner compulsion made him do so. The captain said nothing this time, and the Australian section of the crowd began to barrack. That is to say they shouted unpleasant remarks, and some of them asked the captain where he had found the boy, and if he had played cricket before. Probably the barracker that shouted that had meant to exaggerate, and would have been astonished himself, had he been told how seldom Porlick had ever played. A suspicion came over Porlick's mind that the Devil was laughing at him. And what was particularly annoying was that the Devil seemed to be making himself out to be in the right and Porlick in the wrong. For the Devil was keeping his promise of a wicket for every ball, while Porlick, though getting two wickets in the two first balls of a Test Match, was being made to look ridiculous. Another batsman was coming in. "Don't play any football with him," shouted somebody in the crowd. Porlick could only do his best, which was a very trifling thing compared to the Devil's worst. And into the next ball the Devil seemed indeed to have put his worst; for it went ill-pitched and wide and absurdly slow. The batsman did not even attempt to reach it, as it trickled wide past the wicket. He turned instead to the captain, who was fielding on the leg side, and pointed his bat at him and asked him, "Is this cricket we're playing?"

'The English captain hardly knew what to answer. But the Australian in turning had moved his right foot, and when he lifted his bat to point with it he was out of his ground, and the wicket-keeper, just able to reach the ball that was trickling by, picked it up and put down the wicket. Porlick had got the hat-trick now, and a roar went up from the ground such as you might expect when a hat-trick was scored at a Test Match. And yet it was not the right kind of roar. There was a snarl in it. The captain and one or two others came together and talked. But they said nothing to Porlick. The next batsman walked in, looking as if he were wondering, and took some time over patting the block, as though it mattered where he put his bat against such bowling as that. And then Porlick bowled again. Up went the ball even higher into the air than the first, and when it began to drop it was clear that it would come down beyond the wicket, nearer to the wicket-keeper than to the batsman. But it was not out of the batsman's reach, and by stepping back he was able to hit it, and he hit it hard and it went clear to the boundary, never touching the ground on the way. The whole crowd cheered, not only because they liked a good hit, but because everyone in it felt it was time that the Australians had a chance. But in stepping back at that wild ball the Australian had trod on his wicket, and he was out like the rest; and there were four wickets down for no runs. The Australian captain walked out of the pavilion to talk to the English captain, but thought better of it when he had gone a few yards, and turned back. For after all there was nothing that he could say. A cluster of the English team stood round the captain talking. And then another Australian came to the wicket. He grimly patted the block and looked towards the bowler. And there came another of those kite-like balls, soaring up in the air and over the wicket, and dropping towards the wicket-keeper's hands. And the bats-man, obviously in a temper, hit at it with his bat in one hand. And that ill-tempered blow at the ball caught the wicket-keeper on the head. It dropped him, and the ball went on, and the batsmen began to run a bye. But there came an appeal from Porlick for interfering with the field, and the umpire, taking the view that the hasty blow was intentional, gave the batsman out.

' "Well, it works all right," said Porlick aloud.

' "What works?" said mid-off.

' "Nothing," said Porlick.

'The temper of the crowd was now nasty, and all those who were unaware that you did not take a bowler off in the middle of an over were shouting, "Take him off." The wicket-keeper got to his feet again. Some of the English fielders were looking towards the captain, wondering what he would do. "There's only one more ball to go," he said to one of them. Then the Australian captain came in. He took his stand and looked queerly at Porlick and Porlick bowled. This time the ball bumped half-way down the pitch and trickled along it and was obviously not going to reach the wicket. "We've come to play cricket," said the Australian captain, and stepped out and picked up the ball and threw it back at the bowler.

'Porlick appealed, and the umpire had no option but to give the Australian captain out for handling the ball. Of course the Australian should not have done it, but tempers were running high and it was one of those things that can happen on such occasions. Then the umpire said "Over", and the English captain gave a sigh. He walked all the way to the pavilion with the Australian captain, apologising. And he put Porlick far out in the deep field, and the next over was bowled like an over during a Test Match. The first ball that came to Porlick he let go by, whether or not he was enough of a fielder to have been able to stop it, and he ran after it under the railings among the crowd, and was never seen in Hawnby again. He hadn't much money left by then, and he walked most of the way home. He had seven magical balls left, but I never knew what he did with them. I rather think he became afraid of a cricket-ball and never touched one again. The Australians, in spite of their losses, managed somehow to make a draw of it.'

'What was the date of that match?' asked Terbut.

'Porlick never told me,' said Jorkens. 'But what he did tell me was that the Press hushed the whole thing up. And so they would. You don't see attacks on archbishops in English papers. And, though I don't say that cricket has the sanctity of an archbishop, it is our national game, and the Test is the supreme example of it. No use in showing it in a ridiculous light. So the whole thing was hushed up here, and the Press in Australia co-operated. And foreign countries are uninterested in cricket in any case.'

'But it was played at Hawnby?' asked Terbut.

'Certainly,' said Jorkens, 'but they never played there again after that match. I hear they have let the whole ground go back to moor. I believe it's nothing but heather now. Even the pavilion fell in and is covered with it. And as for cricketers, there are only grouse.

'But never trust the Devil. He doesn't play fair. Porlick paid a perfectly good virtue, which he never got back; and though the letter of the bargain was kept, he got nothing worth having for it. Never trust him, Terbut.'

'Considering where you first introduced us, as it were, to your friend Porlick,' said Terbut, 'he does not sound a very virtuous young man. Can you tell us what virtue he gave in exchange for those wickets?'

'That of always speaking the truth,' said Jorkens.

The Rabbits

by A. A. MILNE

Although A. A. Milne insisted he was no more than a moderate cricketer, his many contributions about the sport to Punch *over the years would make him another entertaining companion for the team. And any chance to spend some time with a man who created the immortal Winnie-the-Pooh and his friends would surely be something not to be missed.*

Milne's regard for the lighter side of the game can be found in his books such as Cricket and Other Verse, The Luncheon Interval *and* The Day's Play, *in all of which he gives hints about some of the games he himself played in and around the southern counties. 'The Rabbits' is an outstanding example of his talent for comedy writing and also reveals his ear for the foibles of humanity. It evocatively recreates a typical 1930s 'cricket week' in the country with a group of 'bright young things'. What makes this amusing tale even funnier is the cricket play which the group stage as their finale to the week. Milne was, of course, a celebrated playwright, too, and one wonders if he didn't secretly nurse the ambition to put a cricketing production on the London stage.*

1

'By Hobbs,' cried Archie, as he began to put away the porridge, 'I feel as fit as anything this morning. I'm absolutely safe for a century.'

'You shouldn't boast with your mouth full,' Myra told her brother.

'It wasn't quite full,' pleaded Archie, 'and I really am good for runs to-day.'

'You will make', I said, 'exactly fourteen.'

'Hallo, good morning. Didn't see you were there.'

'I have been here all the time. Fourteen.'

'It seems a lot,' said Myra doubtfully.

Archie laughed in scorn.

'The incoming batsman,' I began, 'who seemed in no way daunted by the position of affairs—'

'Five hundred for nine,' put in Myra.

'—reached double figures for the fourth time this season, with a lofty snick to the boundary. Then turning his attention to the slow bowler he despatched him between his pads and the wicket for a couple. This, however, was his last scoring stroke, as in the same over he played forward to a long hop and fell victim to the vigilance of the wicket-keeper.'

'For nearly a quarter of an hour,' continued Myra, 'he had defied the attack, and the character of his batting may be easily judged from the fact that his score included one five—'

'Four from an overthrow,' I added in parenthesis.

'And one four. Save for a chance to mid-on before he had scored, and another in the slips when seven, his innings was almost entirely free from blemish—'

'Although on one occasion he had the good fortune, when playing back to a half-volley, to strike the wicket without dislodging the bails.'

'See to-morrow's *Sportsman*,' concluded Myra.

'Oh, you children,' laughed Archie, as he walked over to inspect the ham. 'Bless you.'

Miss Fortescue gave a little cough and began to speak. Miss Fortescue is one of those thoroughly good girls who take an interest in everything. A genuine trier. On this occasion she said: 'I often wonder who it is who writes those accounts in the *Sportsman*.'

'It is believed to be Mr Simpson,' said Archie.

Simpson looked up with a start, and jerked his glasses into his tea. He fished them out and wiped them thoughtfully.

'The credible', he began, 'is rarely—'

'Gentlemen, I pray you silence for Mr Simpson's epigram,' cried Archie.

'Oh, I always thought Mr Simpson wrote verses in the *Saturday Review*,' said Miss Fortescue in the silence which followed.

'As a relaxation only,' I explained. 'The other is his life-work. We read him with great interest; that bit about the heavy roller being requisitioned is my favourite line.'

'Mr Simpson and Killick and Crawford all play in glasses,'
put in Myra eagerly, across the table.

'That is their only point in common,' added Archie.

'Oh, isn't he a very good player?'

'Well, he's a thoroughly honest and punctual and sober
player,' I said, 'but—the fact is, he and I and the Major don't
make many runs nowadays. We generally give, as he has
said in one of his less popular poems, a local habitation to
the—er—airy nothing.'

'I thought it was Shakespeare said that.'

'Shakespeare or Simpson. Hallo, there's Thomas at last.'

Thomas is in the Admiralty, which is why he is always
late. It is a great pity that he was christened Thomas; he can
never rise to the top of his profession with a name like
that. You couldn't imagine a Thomas McKenna—or even a
Thomas Nelson, but he doesn't seem to mind somehow.

'Morning, everybody,' said Thomas. 'Isn't it a beastly
day?'

'We'll hoist the south cone for you,' said Archie, and he
balanced a mushroom upside down on the end of his fork.

'What's the matter with the day?' asked our host, the
Major, still intent on his paper.

'It's so early.'

'When I was a boy—'

'My father, Major Mannering,' said Archie, 'will now
relate an anecdote of Waterloo.'

But the Major was deep in his paper. Suddenly he—there
is only one word for it—snorted.

'The Budget,' said Myra and Archie, exchanging anxious
glances.

'Ha, that's good,' he said, 'that's very good! "If the Chancellor of the Exchequer imagines that he can make his iniquitous Budget more acceptable to a disgusted public by treating
it in a spirit of airy persiflage he is at liberty to try. But airy
persiflage, when brought into contact with the determined
temper of a nation—" '

'Who *is* the hairy Percy, anyhow?' said Thomas to himself.

The Major glared at the interrupter for a moment. Then—
for he knows his weakness, and is particularly fond of
Thomas—he threw his paper down and laughed. 'Well,' he
said, 'are we going to win today?' And while he and Archie
talked about the wicket, his daughter removed *The Times* to
a safe distance.

'But there aren't eleven of you here,' said Miss Fortescue
to me, 'and if you and Mr Simpson and Major Mannering
aren't very good, you'll be beaten. It's against the village the
first two days, isn't it?'

'When I said we weren't very good, I only meant we
didn't make many runs. Mr Simpson is a noted fast bowler,
the Major has a M.C.C. scarf, which can be seen quite easily
at point, and I keep wicket. Between us we dismiss many a
professor. Just as they are shaping for a cut, you know, they
catch sight of the Major's scarf, lose their heads and give me
an easy catch. Then Archie and Thomas take centuries, one
of the gardeners bends them from the off and makes them
swim a bit, the Vicar of his plenty is lending us two sons,
Tony and Dahlia Blair come down this morning, and there
is a chauffeur who plays for keeps. How many is that?'

'Eleven, isn't it?'

'It ought only to be ten,' said Myra, who had overheard.

'Oh yes, I was counting Miss Blair,' said Miss Fortescue.

'We never play more than ten a side,' said Archie.

'Oh, why?'

'So as to give the scorer an extra line or two for the byes.'

Myra laughed; then, catching my eye, looked preternatur-
ally solemn.

'If you've quite finished breakfast, Mr Gaukrodger,' she
said, 'there'll be just time for me to beat you at croquet
before the Rabbits take the field.'

'Right O,' I said.

Of course, you know, my name isn't really Gaukrodger.

2

The Major has taken a great deal of trouble with his ground, and the result pleases everybody. If you are a batsman you applaud the short boundaries; if you are a wicket-keeper (as I am), and Thomas is bowling what he is pleased to call googlies, you have leisure to study some delightful scenery; and if you are a left-handed bowler, with a delivery outside the screen, there is behind you a belt of trees which you cannot fail to admire. When Archie was born, and they announced the fact to the Major, his first question was (so I understand), 'Right or left handed?' They told him 'Left' to quiet him, and he went out and planted a small forest, so that it should be ready for Archibald's action when he grew up. Unfortunately, Archie turned out to be no bowler at all (in my opinion)—and right-handed at that. Nemesis, as the ha'penny papers say.

'Well?' we all asked, when Archie came back from tossing.

'They lost, and put us in.'

'Good man.'

'May I have my sixpence back?' I said. 'You haven't bent it or anything, have you? Thanks.'

As the whole pavilion seemed to be full of people putting on their pads in order to go in first, I wandered outside. There I met Myra.

'Hallo, we're in,' I said. 'Come and sit on the roller with me, and I'll tell you all about Jayes.'

'Can't for a moment. Do go and make yourself pleasant to Dahlia Blair. She's just come.'

'Do you think she'd be interested in Jayes? I mean the Leicestershire cricketer, not the disinfectant. Oh, all right, then I won't.'

I wandered over to the deck-chairs, and exchanged greetings with Miss Blair.

'I have been asked to make myself pleasant,' I said. 'I suppose that means telling you all about everybody, doesn't it?'

'Yes, please.'

'Well, we're in, as you see. That's the Vicar leading his team out. He's no player really—one of the "among others we noticed". But he's a good father, and we've borrowed two offsprings from him. Here comes Archie and Wilks. Wilks drove you from the station, I expect?'

'He did. And very furiously.'

'Well, he hardly drives at all, when he's in. He's terribly slow—what they call Nature's reaction. Archie, you will be sorry to hear, has just distinguished himself by putting me in last. He called it ninth wicket down, but I worked it out, and there doesn't seem to be anybody after me. It's simply spite.'

'I hope Mr Archie makes some runs,' said Dahlia. 'I don't mind so much about Wilks, you know.'

'I'm afraid he is only going to make fourteen today. That's the postman going to bowl to him. He has two deliveries, one at 8 a.m. and one at 12.30 p.m.—the second one is rather doubtful. Archie always takes guard with the bail, you observe, and then looks round to see if we're all watching.'

'Don't be so unkind.'

'I'm annoyed,' I said, 'and I intensely dislike the name Archibald. Ninth wicket down!'

The umpire having called 'Play,' Joe, the postman, bounded up to the wicket and delivered the ball. Archie played forward with the easy confidence of a school professional when nobody is bowling to him. And then the leg-bail disappeared.

'Oh!' cried Dahlia. 'He's out!'

I looked at her, and I looked at Archie's disconsolate back as he made for the pavilion; and I knew what he would want. I got up.

'I must go now,' I said. 'I've promised to sit on the heavy roller for a bit. Archie will be here in a moment. Will you tell him from me that we both thought he wasn't quite ready for that one, and that it never rose an inch? Thank you very much.'

I discovered Myra, and we sat on the roller together.

'Well, I've been making myself pleasant,' I said. 'And then when Archie got out I knew he'd want to sit next to her, so I came away. That is what they call tact in *The Lady*.'

'Archie *is* rather fond of her,' said Myra. 'I don't know if—'

'Yes, yes, I understand. Years ago—'

'Let's see. Are you ninety or ninety-one? I always forget.'

'Ninety-one next St Crispin's Day. I'm sorry Archie's out. "The popular cricketer was unfortunate enough to meet a trimmer first ball, and the silent sympathy of the Bank Holiday crowd went out to him as he wended his way to the Pavilion." Extract from "*Pavilions I have wended to*, by Percy Benskin." Help! There goes Blair!'

After this the situation became very serious. In an hour seven of us had got what I might call the postman's knock. Wilks was still in, but he had only made nine. The score was fifty-two, thanks entirely to Simpson, who had got thirty-five between first and second slip in twenty minutes. This stroke of his is known as the Simpson upper cut, and is delivered straight from the shoulder and off the edge of the bat.

'This is awful,' said Myra. 'You'll simply have to make some now.'

'I think it's time Wilks got on to his second speed. Why doesn't somebody tell him? Hallo, there goes John. I knew there wasn't a run there. Where are my gloves?'

'You mustn't be nervous. Oh, *do* make some.'

'The condemned man walked firmly to the wickets. "What is that, umpire?" he asked in his usual cool voice. "Houtside the leg stump, sir," said the man in white. "Good," he replied. . . . What an ass your second gardener is. Fancy being potted out like that, just as if he were a geranium. I ought to wear a cap, oughtn't I, in case I want to bow when I come in. Goodbye; I shall be back for lunch, I expect.'

I passed Joe on my way to the wickets, and asked pleasantly after his wife and family. He was rather brusque about it, and sent down a very fast half-volley which kept low. Then Wilks and I returned to the pavilion together amid cheers. On the whole, the Rabbits had lived up to their reputation.

'Well, we *are* a lot of bunnies,' said Archie at lunch. 'Joe simply stands there looking like a lettuce and out we all trot. We shall have to take to halma or something. Simpson, you swim, don't you?'

'You don't have to swim at halma,' said Simpson.

'Anyhow,' said Blair, 'we can't blame the Selection Committee.'

'I blame Thomas,' I said. 'He would have eight, and he wouldn't wait. I don't blame myself, because my average is now three spot five, and yesterday it was only three spot one.'

'That is impossible, if you made nought today,' said Simpson eagerly.

'Not if I divided it wrong yesterday.'

'Averages,' said the Major to the Vicar, catching the last sentence but two, 'are the curse of modern cricket. When I was a boy—'

'This,' Archie explained to us, 'takes us back to the thirties, when Felix Mynn bowled Ensign Mannering with a full pitch.'

'Dear old Fuller Pitch. Ah! what do they know of England, who only King and Jayes?' I declaimed. 'Libretto by Simpson.'

'Who's finished?' said Archie, getting up. 'Come out and smoke. Now, we simply must buck up and out the opposition. Simpson ought to bump them at Joe's end, and Thomas—'

'I always swerve after lunch,' said Thomas.

'I don't wonder. What I was going to say was that you would box them in the slips. You know, if we all buck up—'

We bucked up and outed them at the end of the day for 250.

3

'Will somebody give me a cigarette,' said Myra, stretching out a hand.

'I fancy not,' I said. 'Thomas and I both feel that you are too young.'

'I don't really want one, but when I'm locked up in the billiard-room with two dumb men—'

'We were reflecting on our blessed victory.'

'Were you thinking of Archie's century or John's bowling?'

'Neither, oddly enough. I was recalling my own catch which won the match. Poetry; let's go and tell Simpson.'

'It *was* a skier,' said Myra. 'I thought it was never coming down. What did you think of all the time?'

'Everything. All my past life flashed before my eyes. I saw again my happy childhood's days, when I played innocently in the—er—pantry. I saw myself at school, sl—working. I saw—'

'Did you happen,' interrupted Thomas, when we both thought he was fast asleep, 'to see yourself being badly taken on by me at billiards?'

'Thomas, you're not properly awake, old friend. I know that feeling. Turn over on the other side and take a deep breath.'

Thomas rose and stretched himself, and went over to the cue rack. 'You should have heard him siding about his blessed billiards this morning,' he told Myra.

'I didn't side. I simply said that anybody could beat Thomas. Do they play billiards much at the Admiralty? I should have thought the motion—'

'Take a cue. Myra will mark.'

'Rather; I can mark like anything.'

'Once upon a time,' I said, 'there was a laddy who wanted

to get into the Admiralty. But his mother said, "Not until you have learnt to swim, Thomas." So he had a set of six private lessons for one guinea before he went in for the examination. He came out thirty-eighth, and was offered a lucrative appointment in the post office. . . . Hence his enormous skill at billiards. Thick or clear?'

'I will adventure half a crown upon the game,' said Thomas, giving a miss.

'Right O, Rothschild. Now, are you ready, marker? I'm spot. Hadn't you better oil the board a bit? Well, as long as you can work it quickly enough.'

I took careful aim, and my ball went up the table and back again, with the idea, I imagine, of inspecting the wicket. It seemed quite fast.

'One all,' said Myra, and Thomas kindly brought his ball and mine to the top of the table.

'I fancy I shall be able to swerve from this end,' I said. I tried a delicate cannon, and just missed the object ball. 'I shall find a spot directly—there's one under the red ball, I believe.'

'Do try and hit something,' said Myra.

'The marker is not allowed to give advice,' I said sternly. 'What's the matter, Thomas?'

'I'm not quite sure what to do.'

'I think you ought to chalk your cue here,' I said, after examining the position.

'I've done that.'

'Then ram the red.'

Thomas rammed and all but sank it in the left-hand pocket.

'I am now,' I said, 'going to do a cannon off the cushion. Marker, what is my score?'

'One, sir.'

'Then kindly get ready to put it up to three. . . . Rotten luck.'

'Wrong side,' said Myra judicially.

'No, I meant to hit it that side.'

'I mean it wanted a little running side.'

'This isn't Queen's Club. Go on, Thomas.'

Thomas, who had been chalking his cue, advanced to the table. 'Hallo,' he said, 'where's the other ball?'

I looked at the table, and there were only two balls on it!

'That's an extraordinary thing,' I said in amazement. 'I'm almost certain we started with three.'

'Did you put me down?'

'Certainly not; I shouldn't dream of doing such a thing. I don't say I mayn't have slipped down myself when nobody was looking. Myra, did you notice which pocket I was trying for that time?'

We felt in all of them, and at last found my ball in one of the bottom ones. It must have gone there very quietly.

'Score, marker?' I asked confidently, as I prepared to continue my break.

'Oh, you're going over the crease,' cried Myra.

I took my ball back an inch. '*Will* you tell me the score?' I said.

'Stevenson (in play) three; Inman, two. Inman's two were both wides.'

Barely were the words out of her mouth when Inman's score was increased by a no-ball. A miss-cue they call it technically.

'Three all,' said Myra. 'This is awfully exciting. First one is ahead, and then the other.'

'By the way, how many up are we playing?'

'Five, aren't you?' said Myra.

This roused Thomas. He had played himself in, and now proceeded to make a pretty break of seventeen. I followed. There was a collision off the middle pocket between spot and red, and both went down. Then plain was unintentionally sunk as the result of a cannon shot, and spot and red sailed into harbour. With Thomas's miss I scored eleven. Unfortunately, off my next stroke, Thomas again went down.

'Billiards,' he said.

'You don't think I want to put the rotten thing down, do you? It's such a blessed rabbit. Directly it sees a hole anywhere it makes for it. Hallo, six more. I shall now give what they call a miss in baulk.'

'Oh, good miss,' cried Myra, as spot rested over the middle pocket.

'That was a googly. You both thought it would break the other way.'

The game went on slowly. When Thomas was ninety and I was ninety-nine, there was a confused noise without, and Archie and Miss Blair burst into the room. At least only Archie actually burst; Miss Blair entered sedately.

'Who's winning?' cried Archie.

'What an absurd question,' I said. 'As if we should tell you.'

'All right. Dahl—Miss Blair, have you ever seen billiards played really well?'

'Never.'

'Then now's your chance. Ninety-ninety-nine—they've only just begun. This is Thomas's first break, I expect. There—he's got a clear board. You get five extra for that, and the other man is rubiconed. Ninety-nine all. Now, it is only a question of who misses first.'

I put down my cue.

'Thomas,' I began, 'we have said some hard things about each other tonight, but when I listen to Archie I feel very friendly towards you.'

'Archibald', said Thomas, 'is a beastly name.'

'So I told Miss Blair. For a man who was, so to speak, born with a silver billiard-table in his mouth to come here and make fun of two persevering and, in my case, promising players is—'

'You'll never finish that sentence,' said Myra. 'Try some more billiards.'

'It was almost impossible to say what I wanted to say grammatically,' I answered, and I hit my ball very hard up the table at the white.

'It's working across,' said Archie, after the second bounce; 'it must hit the red soon. I give it three more laps.'

'It's going much more slowly now,' said Miss Blair.

'Probably it's keeping a bit of a sprint for the finish. Wait till it gets its second wind. No, I'm afraid it's no good; it ought to have started sooner. Hallo, yes, it's—got him!'

'It hasn't finished yet,' I said calmly. 'Look—there!'

'Jove!' said Archie, shaking my hand, 'that's the longest loser I've ever seen. My dear old man, what a performer. The practice you must have had. The years you must have devoted to the game. I wonder—could you *possibly* spare an hour or two tomorrow to play cricket for us?'

4

A hundred and eighty for none. The umpire waved his lily hand, and the scorer entered one more 'four' in his book. Seeing that the ball had gone right through a bicycle which was leaning up against the pavilion, many people (the owner of the bicycle, anyhow) must have felt that the actual signalling of a boundary was unnecessary; but our umpire is a stickler for the etiquette of the game. Once when—But no, on second thoughts, I shan't tell you that story. You would say it was a lie—as indeed it is.

'Rotten,' said Archie to me, as we crossed over. (A good captain always confides in his wicket-keeper.)

'Don't take Simpson off,' I said. 'I like watching him.'

'I shall go on again myself soon.'

'Oh, it's not so bad as that. Don't lose heart.'

The score was 200 when we met again.

'I once read a book by a lady', I said, 'in which the hero started the over with his right hand and finished it with his left. I suppose Simpson couldn't do that?'

'He's a darned rotten bowler, anyway.'

'His direction is all right, but his metre is so irregular.'

At the end of the next over, 'What shall I do?' asked Archie in despair.

'Put the wicket-keeper on,' I said at once.

The idea was quite a new one to him. He considered it for a moment.

'Can you bowl?' he said at last.

'No.'

'Then what on earth—'

'Look here; you've tried 'em with people who *can* bowl, and they've made 220 in an hour and a half; somebody who can't bowl will be a little change for them. That's one reason. The second is that we shall all have a bit of a rest while I'm taking my things off. The third is that I bet Myra a shilling—'

Archie knelt down, and began to unbuckle my pads. 'I'll "keep" myself,' he said. 'Are you fast or slow?'

'I haven't the faintest idea. Just as it occurs to me at the moment, I expect.'

'Well, you're quite right; you can't be worse than some of us. Will you have a few balls down first?'

'No, thanks; I should like to come as a surprise to them.'

'Well, pitch 'em up anyhow.'

'I shall probably vary my length—if possible without any alteration of action.'

I am now approaching the incredible. The gentle reader, however, must not be nasty about it; he should at least pretend to believe, and his best way of doing this is to listen very silently to what follows. When he has heard my explanation I shall assume that he understands.

Bowling is entirely a question of when you let go of the ball. If you let go too soon the result is a wide over the batsman's head; if too late, a nasty crack on your own foot. Obviously there are spaces in between. By the law of averages one must let go at the right moment at least once. Why not then at the first ball? And in the case of a person like myself, who has a very high action and a good mouth—I mean who has a very high delivery, such a ball (after a week of Simpsons and Archies) would be almost unplayable.

Very well, then; I did let go at the right moment, but, unfortunately, I took off from the wrong crease. Then

umpire's cry of 'No-ball' and the shattering of the Quidnunc's wicket occurred simultaneously.

'Good ball,' said Archie. 'Oh, bad luck!'

I tried to look as though, on the whole, I preferred it that
way—as being ultimately more likely to inspire terror in the
batsman at my end. Certainly, it gave me confidence; made
me over-confident in fact, so that I held on to the next ball
much too long, and it started bouncing almost at once.

The Quidnunc, who was convinced by this that he had
been merely having a go at the previous ball, shouldered his
bat and sneered at it. He was still sneering when it came in
very quickly, and took the bottom of the leg-stump. (Finger
spin, chiefly.)

Archie walked up slowly, and gazed at me.

'Well?' I said jauntily.

'No, don't speak. I just want to look, and look, and look.
It's wonderful. No elastic up the sleeve, or anything.'

'This is where it first pitched,' said the Major, as he examined the ground.

'Did you think of letting in a brass tablet?' I inquired
shortly.

'He is quite a young man,' went on Archie dreamily, 'and
does not care to speak about his plans for the future. But he
is of opinion that—'

'Break, break, break,' said Simpson. 'Three altogether.'

'Look here, is there anybody else who wants to say anything? No? Then I'll go on with my over.'

Archie, who had begun to walk back to his place, returned
thoughtfully to me.

'I just wanted to say, old chap, that if you're writing home
tonight about it, you might remember me to your people.'

Blair was about the only person who didn't insult me.
This was because he had been fielding long-on; and as soon
as the wicket fell he moved round about fifty yards to talk
to Miss Fortescue. What people can see in her—Well, directly
my next ball was bowled he started running as hard as he

could to square-leg, and brought off one of the finest catches I've ever seen.

'The old square-leg trap,' said Archie. 'But you cut it rather fine, didn't you? I suppose you knew he was a sprinter?'

'I didn't cut it at all—I was bowling. Go away.'

Yes, I confess it. I did the hat-trick. It was a good length half-volley, and the batsman, who had watched my first three balls, was palpably nervous. Archie walked round and round me in silence for some time, and then went over to Thomas.

'He's playing tennis with me this evening,' he began.

'I was beaten at billiards by him last night,' said Thomas proudly.

'He's going to let me call him by his Christian name.'

'They say he's an awfully good chap when you know him,' replied Thomas.

I got another wicket with the last ball of the over, and then we had lunch. Myra was smiling all over her face when we came in, but beyond a 'Well bowled, Walter' (which I believe to be Brearley's name), would have nothing to do with me. Instead she seized Archie, and talked long and eagerly to him. And they both laughed a good deal.

'Arkwright,' I heard Archie say at the end. 'He's sure to be there, and would do it like a shot.'

Like a wise captain Archie did not put me on after lunch, and Simpson soon began to have the tail in difficulties. Just after the eighth wicket fell a telegram came out. Archie took it and handed it to me. 'From Maclaren, I expect,' he said with a grin.

'You funny ass; I happen to know it's from Dick. I asked him for a wire about the Kent match.'

'Oh, did Kent win?' said Archie, looking over my shoulder. As I opened it, the others came up, and I read—

'Please be in attendance for next Test Match.

'Hawke.'

I got three more that afternoon. One from Fry, one from Leveson-Gower, and one from Maclaren. They all came from Lord's, and I've half a mind to take my telegrams with me, and go. Then Myra would probably get six months in the second division.

'But I shouldn't mind *that*,' said Myra. 'You could easily bowl—I mean bail—me out.'

A silly joke, I call it.

5

I selected a handkerchief, gave a last look at the weather, which was beastly, and went down (very late) to breakfast. As I opened the door there was a sudden hush. Everybody looked eagerly at me. Then Miss Fortescue tittered.

Well, you know how one feels when that happens. I put my hand quickly to my tie—it was still there. I squinted down my nose, but there was no smut. To make quite sure I went over to the glass. Then Simpson exploded.

Yet nobody spoke. They all sat there watching me, and at last I began to get nervous. I opened my mouth to say 'Good morning,' but before I got it out Miss Blair gave a little shriek of excitement. That upset me altogether. I walked up to the teapot, and pouring myself out a cup said, with exaggerated carelessness, 'Rotten day, isn't it?'

And then came the laughter—shout after shout.

I held out my hand to Myra. 'Goodbye,' I said, 'I'm going home. Thank you for a very jolly time, but I'm not going to be bullied.'

'Oh, you dear,' she gurgled.

'I *am* rather sweet before breakfast,' I admitted, 'but how—'

'It was too heavenly of you. I never thought you would.'

'I think I shall go back to bed.'

'It was rather rough luck,' said Archie, 'but of course the later you are, the worse it is for you.'

'And the higher the fewer. Quite so. If this is from Breakfast Table Topics in the *Daily Mirror*, I haven't seen them today; but I'll do my best.'

'Archie, explain.'

Archie took up a piece of paper from the table, and explained. 'It's like this,' he said. 'I came down first and looked at the weather, and said—'

'Any one would,' I put in quickly.

'Well, then, Blair came in and said, "Beastly day," and then Simpson—Well, I thought I'd write down everybody's first remark, to see if anybody let the weather alone. Here they are.'

'It's awful,' put in Myra, 'to have one's remarks taken down straight off. I've quite forgotten what I said.'

This was the list:

Archie: 'Bother.' (So he says.)

Blair: 'What a beastly day!'

Simpson: 'What a jolly day!'

The Major: 'Well, not much cricket today, hey?'

Myra: 'Oh dear, what a day!'

Miss Blair: 'What a terrible day!'

Miss Fortescue: 'Oh, you *poor* men—*what* a day!'

Thomas: 'Rotten day, isn't it?'

Me: 'Rotten day, isn't it?'

'I don't think much of Thomas's remark,' I said.

Later on in the morning we met (all except the Major, that is) in the room which Myra calls hers and Archie calls the nursery, and tried to think of something to do.

'I'm not going to play bridge all day for anyone,' said Archie.

'The host should lay himself out to amuse his guests,' said Myra.

'Otherwise, his guests will lay him out,' I warned him, 'to amuse themselves.'

'Well, what do you all want to do?'

'I should like to look at a photograph album,' said Thomas.

'Stump cricket.'

'What about hide-and-seek?'

'No, I've got it,' cried Archie; 'we'll be boy scouts.'

'Hooray!' cried everybody else.

Archie was already on his hands and knees. 'Ha!' he said, 'is that the spoor of the white ant that I see before me? Spoorly not. I have but been winded by the water-beetle.

> 'Sound, sound the trumpet, beat the drum,
>   To all the scouting world proclaim
> One crowded stalk upon the tum
>   Is worth an age without a name.

'Archie!' shrieked Myra in horror. 'It is too late,' she added, 'all the ladies have swooned.'

We arranged sides. Myra and I and Simpson and Thomas against the others. They were to start first.

'This isn't simply hide-and-seek,' said Archie, as they went off. 'You've got to track us fairly. We shall probably "blaze" door-posts. When you hear the bleat of a tinned sardine that means we're ready. Keep your eyes skinned, my hearties, and heaven defend the right.'

'We ought to have bare knees really,' said Myra, when they'd gone. 'Boy scouts always do. So that when they go through a bed of nettles they know they've been.'

'I shall stalk the stairs to begin with,' I said. 'Simpson, you go down the back way and look as much like a vacuum-cleaner as possible. Then they won't notice you. Thomas and Myra—Hush! Listen! Was that the bleat of a fresh sardine or the tinned variety?'

'Tinned,' said Myra. 'Let's go.'

We went. I took the Queen Anne staircase on my—in the proper stalking position. I moved very slowly, searching for spoor. Half-way down the stairs my back fin slipped and I shot over the old oak at a tremendous pace, landing in the hall like a Channel swimmer. Looking up, I saw Thomas in front of me. He was examining the door for 'blazes'. Myra was next to him, her ear to the ground, listening for the gallop of horses' hoofs. I got up and went over to them.

'Hast seen aught of a comely wench in parlous case, hight Miss Dahlia?' I asked Thomas.

'Boy scouts don't talk like that,' he said gruffly.

'I beg your pardon. I was thinking that I was a Cavalier and you were a Roundhead. Now I perceive that you are just an ordinary fathead.'

'Why,' said Myra at the foot of the stairs, 'what does this button mean? Have I found a clue?'

I examined it and then I looked at my own coat.

'You have,' I said. 'Somebody has been down those stairs quite recently, for the button is still warm.'

'Where is Scout Simpson?'

At that moment he appeared breathless with excitement.

'I have had an adventure,' he said hurriedly, without saluting. 'I was on the back stairs looking like a vacuum-cleaner when suddenly Archie and Miss Blair appeared. They looked right at me, but didn't seem to penetrate my disguise. Archie, in fact, leant against me, and said to Miss Blair: "I will now tell you of my secret mission. I carry caviare—I mean despatches—to the general. Breathe but a word of this to the enemy, and I miss the half-holiday on Saturday. Come, let us be going, but first to burn the secret code." And—and then he struck a match on me, and burned it.'

Myra gurgled and hastily looked solemn again. 'Proceed, Scout Simpson,' she said, 'for the night approaches apace.'

'Well, then they started down the stairs, and I went after them on my—scouting, you know. I made rather a noise at one corner, and Archie looked round at me, and said to Miss Blair: "The tadpoles are out full early. See yonder where one lies basking." And he came back, and put his foot on me and said, "Nay, 'tis but a shadow. Let us return right hastily. Yet tarry a moment, what time I lay a false trail." So they tarried and he wrote a note and dropped it on me. And, afterward, I got up and here it is.'

'The secret despatch,' cried Myra.

'It's addressed to the Scoutmistress, and it says outside: "Private, not to be opened till Christmas Day." '

Myra opened it and read: 'Your blessed scouts are every-where. Let me have five minutes with her in the nursery, there's a dear. I'd do as much for you.'

But she didn't read it aloud, and I didn't see it till some time afterwards. She simply put it away, and smiled, and announced that the scouts would now adjourn to the billiard-room for pemmican and other refreshments; which they did. The engagement was announced that evening.

6

'Well,' said Thomas, 'how are we going to celebrate the joyful event?'

We were sitting on the lawn, watching Blair and Miss Fortescue play croquet. Archie and Dahlia were not with us; they had (I suppose) private matters to discuss. Our match did not begin for another hour, happily for the lovers; hap-pily also for the croquet-players, who had about fifty-six hoops, posts, flags and what not to negotiate.

'It's awfully difficult to realise it,' said Myra. 'My own brother! Just fancy—I can hardly believe it.'

'I don't think there can be any doubt,' I said. 'Something's happened to him, anyhow—he's promised to put me in first today.'

'Let's have a dance tomorrow night,' continued Thomas, relentlessly pursuing his original idea. 'And we'll all dance with Miss Blair.'

'Yes. Archie would like that.'

'I remember, some years ago, when I was in Spain,' said Simpson—

'This', I murmured appreciatively, 'is how all the best stories begin.' And I settled myself more comfortably in my chair.

'No,' said Simpson, 'I'm wrong there. It was in Hampstead.' And he returned to his meditations.

'Tell you what,' said Thomas, 'you ought to write 'em an ode, Simpson.'

'There's nothing that rhymes with the lady.'

'There's hair,' I said quite unintentionally.

'I meant with Dahlia.'

'My dear man, there are heaps. Why, there's azalea.'

'That's only one.'

'Well, there are lots of different kinds of azalea.'

'Any rhymes for Archie and Mannering?' said Simpson scornfully.

'Certainly. And Simpson. You might end with him—

> "Forgive the way the metre limps on,
> It's always like that with Samuel Simpson."

You get the idea?'

'Hush,' said Myra, 'Miss Fortescue has passed under a hoop.'

But it is time that we got on to my innings. Archie managed to win the toss, and, as he had promised, took me in with him. It was the proudest and most nervous moment of my life.

'I've never been in first before,' I said, as we walked to the wickets. 'Is there any little etiquette to observe?'

'Oh, rather. Especially if you're going to take first ball.'

'Oh, there's no doubt about my taking the *first* ball.'

'In that case the thing to remember is, that when the umpire calls "play," the side refusing to play loses the match.'

'Then it all rests on me? Your confidence in me must be immense. I think I shall probably consent to play.'

I obtained guard and took my stand at the wicket. Most cricketers nowadays, I am told, adopt the 'two-eyed stance', but for myself I still stick to the good old two-legged one. It seems to be less wearing. My style, I should observe, blends happily the dash of a Joseph Vine with the patience of a Kenneth Hutchings; and after a long innings I find a glass of—I've forgotten the name of it now, but I know I find it very refreshing.

Being the hero (you will admit that—after my hat-trick)

of this true story, I feel I must describe my innings carefully. Though it only totalled seventeen, there was this to be said for it: it is the only innings of less than a hundred ever made by a hero.

It began with a cut to square leg, for which we ran a forced single, and followed on with a brace of ones in the direction of fine-slip. After that, I stopped the bowler in the middle of his run-up, and signalled to a spectator to move away from the screen. This was a put-up job with Myra, and I rather hoped they would give me something for it, but apparently they didn't. At the end of the over, I went up and talked to Archie. In first-class cricket, the batsmen often do this, and it impresses the spectators immensely.

I said, 'I bet you a shilling I'm out next over.'

He said, 'I won't take you.'

I said, 'Then I huff you,' and went back to my crease.

My next scoring stroke was a two-eyed hook over point's head, and then Archie hit three fours running. I had another short conversation with him, in the course of which I recited two lines from Shakespeare and asked him a small but pointed conundrum, and afterwards I placed the ball cleverly to mid-off, the agility of the fieldsman, however, preventing any increment, unearned or otherwise. Finally, I gave my cap to the umpire, made some more ones, changed my bat, and was caught at the wicket.

'I hit it,' I said, as I walked away. I said it to nobody in particular, but the umpire refused to alter his decision.

'I congratulate you,' said Miss Blair, when I was sitting down again.

'I was just going to do that to you,' I said.

'Oh, but you were kind enough to do that last night.'

'Ah, this is extra. I've just been batting out there with your young man. Perhaps you noticed?'

'Well, I think I must have.'

'Yes. Well, I wanted to tell you that I think he has quite an idea of the game, and that with more experience he would probably be good enough to play for—for Surrey. Second eleven. Yes. At hockey.'

'Thank you so much. You've known him a long time, haven't you?'

'We were babes together, Madam. At least, simultaneously. We actually met at school. He had blue eyes and curly hair, and fought the captain on the very first day. On the second day his hair was still curly, but he had black eyes. On the third day he got into the cricket eleven, and on the fourth he was given his footer cap. Afterwards he sang in the choir, and won the competition for graceful diving. It was not until his second term that the headmaster really began to confide in him. By the way, is this the sort of thing you want?'

'Yes,' smiled Dahlia. 'Something like that.'

'Well, then we went to Cambridge together. He never did much work, but his algebra paper in the Little Go was so brilliant that they offered him the Senior Wranglership. He refused on the ground that it might interfere with his training for the tug-of-war, for which he had just obtained his blue—and—It's a great strain making all this up. Do you mind if I stop now?'

'Of course I know that isn't all true, but he *is* like that, isn't he?'

'He is. He put me in first today.'

'I know you really are fond of him.'

'Lorblessyou—yes.'

'That makes you my friend, too.'

'Of course.' I patted her hand. 'That reminds me—*as* a friend I feel bound to warn you that there is a person about in the neighbourhood called Samuel Simpson who meditates an evil design upon you and yours. In short, a poem. In this he will liken you to the azalea, which I take to be a kind of shrubby plant.'

'Yes?'

'Yes, well, all I want to say is, if he comes round with the hat afterwards, don't put anything in.'

'Poor man,' smiled Dahlia. 'That's his living, isn't it?'

'Yes. That's why I say don't put anything in.'

'I see. Oh, there—he's out. Poor Archie.'

'Are you very sorry?' I said, smiling at her. 'I'm just going, you know.'

'Between ourselves,' I said later to Myra, 'that isn't at all a bad girl.'

'Oh, fancy!'

'But I didn't come to talk about her—I came to talk about my seventeen.'

'Yes, do let's.'

'Yes. Er—you begin.'

7

'May I have a dance?' I asked Miss Blair.

She put her head on one side and considered.

'One, two, three—the next but *five*,' she said.

'Thank you. That sounds a lot; is it only one?'

'You may have two running then, if you like.'

'What about two running, and one hopping, and one really gliding? Four altogether.'

'We'll see,' said Miss Blair gravely.

Myra, who was being very busy, came up and dragged me away.

'I want to introduce you to somebody. I say, have you seen Thomas?'

'It's no earthly good introducing me to Thomas again.'

'He's so important because he thinks the dance was his idea; of course I'd meant to have it all along. There she is— her name's Dora Dalton. I think it's Dora.'

'I shall call her Dora, anyhow.'

I was introduced, and we had a very jolly waltz together. She danced delightfully; and when we had found a comfortable corner she began to talk.

She said, 'Do you play cricket?'

I was rather surprised, but I kept quite cool, and said, 'Yes.'

'My brother's very fond of it. He is very good too. He was playing here yesterday against Mr Mannering's team, and made six, and then the umpire gave him out; but he wasn't out really, and he was very angry. I don't wonder, do you?'

I had a sudden horrible suspicion.

'Did you say your name was Dora—I mean his name was Dalton?'

'Yes. And just because he was angry, which anybody would be, the wicket-keeper was very rude, and told him to go home and—and bake his head.'

'Not bake,' I said gently, my suspicion having now become almost a certainty. 'Boil.'

'Go home, and boil his head,' she repeated indignantly.

'And did he?'

'Did he what?'

'Er—did he understand—I mean, don't you think your brother may have misunderstood? I can't believe that a wicket-keeper would ever demean himself by using the word "boil". Not as you might say *boil*. "Cool his head" was probably the expression—it was a very hot day, I remember. And . . . ah, there's the music beginning again. Shall we go back?'

I am afraid Miss Dalton's version of the incident was not quite accurate.

What had happened was this: I had stumped the fellow, when he was nearly a mile-and-a-half outside his crease; and when he got back to it some minutes later, and found the umpire's hand up, he was extremely indignant and dramatic about it. Quite to myself, *sotto voce* as it were, I murmured, 'Oh, go home!' and I may have called attention in some way to the 'bails'. But as to passing any remarks about boiling heads—well, it simply never occurred to me.

I had a dance with Myra shortly after this. She had been

so busy and important that I felt quite a stranger. I adapted my conversation accordingly.

'It's a very jolly floor, isn't it?' I said, as I brought her an ice.

'Oh yes!' said Myra in the same spirit.

'Have you been to many floors—I mean dances, lately?'

'Oh yes!'

'So have I. I think dances have been very late lately. I think when the floor's nice it doesn't matter about the ices. Don't you think the band is rather too elastic—I mean keeps very good time? I think so long as the time is good, it doesn't matter about the floor.'

'Oh, *isn't* it?' said Myra enthusiastically.

There was a pleasant pause while we both thought of something else to say.

'Have you?' we began.

'I beg your pardon,' we said at once.

'I was going to say,' Myra went on, 'have you read any nice books lately, or are you fonder of tennis?'

'I like reading nice books *about* tennis,' I said. 'If they *are* nice books, and are really about tennis. Er—do you live in London?'

'Yes. It is so handy for the theatres, isn't it? There is no place exactly like London, is there? I mean it's so different.'

'Well, of course, up in Liverpool we do get the trams, you know, now. . . . I say, I'm tired of pretending I've only just met you. Let's talk properly.'

At this moment we heard a voice say, 'Let's try in here,' and Archie and Dahlia appeared.

'Hallo! here's the happy pair,' said Myra.

They came in and looked at us diffidently. I leant back and gazed at the ceiling.

'Were you just going?' said Archie.

'We were not,' I said.

'Then we'll stay and talk to you.'

'We were in the middle of an important conversation.'

'Oh, don't mind us.'

'Thank you. It's really for your benefit, so you'd better listen. Let me see, where were we? Oh yes, "One pound of beef, ninepence; three pounds of potatoes, fourpence; one piece of emery paper for the blancmange, tuppence; one pound of india-rubber—" '

' "Dahlia *darling*" ' interrupted Myra, in a fair imitation of Archie's voice, ' "how often have I told you that we *can't* afford india-rubber in the cake? Just a few raisins and a cherry is really all you want. You *musn't* be so extravagant." '

' "Dearest, I do try; and after all, love, it wasn't *I* who fell into the cocoa last night." '

' "I didn't fall in, I simply dropped my pipe in, and it was *you* insisted on pouring it away afterwards. And then, look at this—*One yard of lace*, 4s. 6d. That's for the cutlets, I suppose. For people in our circumstances paper frillings are *quite* sufficient." '

Archie and Dahlia listened to us with open mouths. Then they looked at each other, and then at us again.

'Is there any more?' asked Archie.

'There's lots more, but we've forgotten it.'

'You aren't ill or anything?'

'We are both perfectly well.'

'How's Miss Dalton?'

'Dora', I said, 'is also well. So is Miss Fortescue and so is Thomas. We are all well.'

'I thought, perhaps—'

'No, there you are wrong.'

'I expect it's just the heat and the excitement,' said Dahlia, with a smile. 'It takes some people like that.'

'I'm afraid you miss our little parable,' said Myra.

'We do. Come on, Dahlia.'

'You'll pardon me, Archibald, but Miss Blair is dancing this with me.'

Archie strongly objected, but I left him with Myra, and took Miss Blair away. We sat on the stairs and thought.

'It has been a lovely week,' said Dahlia.

'It has,' I agreed.

'Perhaps more lovely for me than for you.'

'That's just where I don't agree with you. You know, we think it's greatly over-rated. Falling in love, I mean.'

'Who's "we"?'

'Myra and I. We've been talking it over. That's why we rather dwelt upon the sordid side of it just now. I suppose we didn't move you at all?'

'No,' said Dahlia, 'we're settled.'

'That's exactly it,' I said. 'I should hate to be settled. It's so much more fun like this. Myra quite agrees with me.'

Dahlia smiled to herself. 'But perhaps some day,' she began.

'I don't know. I never look more than a week ahead. "It has been great fun this week, and it will probably be great fun next week." That's my motto.'

'Well, ye—es,' said Miss Blair doubtfully.

8

'Do I know everybody?' I asked Myra towards the end of the dinner, looking round the table.

'I think so,' said Myra. 'If there's anybody you don't see in the window, ask for him.'

'I can see most of them. Who's that tall handsome fellow grinning at me now?'

'Me,' said Archie, smiling across at us.

'Go away,' said Myra. 'Gentlemen shouldn't eavesdrop. This is a perfectly private conversation.'

'You've got a lady on each side of you,' I said heatedly, 'why don't you talk to *them*? It's simply scandalous that Myra and I can't get a moment to ourselves.'

'They're both busy; they won't have anything to say to me.'

'Then pull a cracker with yourself. Surely you can think of something, my lad.'

'He has a very jealous disposition,' said Myra, 'and whenever Dahlia—Bother, he's not listening.'

I looked round the table again to see if I could spy a stranger.

'There's a man over there—who's he? Where this orange is pointing.'

'Oranges don't point. Waggle your knife round. Oh, him? Yes, he's a friend of Archie's—Mr Derry.'

'Who is he? Does he do anything exciting?'

'He does, rather. You know those little riddles in the Christmas crackers?'

'Yes?'

'Yes. Well, he couldn't very well do those, because he's an electrical engineer.'

'But why—'

'No, I didn't. I simply asked you if you knew them. And he plays the piano beautifully, and he's rather a good actor, and he never gets up till about ten. Because his room is next to mine, and you can hear everything, and I can hear him not getting up.'

'That doesn't sound much like an electrical engineer. You ask him suddenly what amperes are a penny, and see if he turns pale. I expect he makes up the riddles, after all. Simpson only does the mottoes, I know. Now talk to Thomas for a bit while I drink my orange.'

Five minutes elapsed, or transpired (whichever it is), before I was ready to talk again. Generally, after an orange, I want to have a bath and go straight off to bed, but this particular one had not been so all-overish as usual.

'Now then,' I said, as I examined the crystallised fruit, 'I'm with you in one minute.'

Myra turned round and looked absently at me.

'I don't know how to begin,' she said to herself.

'The beginning's easy enough,' I explained, as I took a dish of green sweets under my charge, 'it's the knowing when to stop.'

'Can you eat those and listen to something serious?'

'I'll try. . . . Yes, I can eat them all right. Now, let's see if I can listen. . . . Yes, I can listen all right.'

'Then it's this. I've been putting it off as long as I can, but you've got to be told tonight. It's—well—do you know why you're here?'

'Of course I do. Haven't I just been showing you?'

'Well, why are you here?'

'Well, frankly, because I'm hungry, I suppose. Of course, I know that if I hadn't been I should have come in to dinner just the same, but—Hang it, I mean that's the root idea of a dining-room, isn't it? And I *am* hungry. At least I was.'

'Stave it off again with an almond,' said Myra, pushing them along to me. 'What I really meant was why you're here in the house.'

This was much more difficult. I began to consider possible reasons.

'Because you all love me,' I started; 'because you put the wrong address on the envelope; because the regular boot-boy's ill; because you've never heard me sing in church; because—stop me when I'm getting warm—because Miss Fortescue refused to come unless I was invited; because—'

'Stop,' said Myra. 'That was it. And, of course, you know I didn't mean that at all.'

'What an awful lot of things you don't mean tonight. Be brave, and have it right out this time.'

'All right, then, I will. One, two, three—we're going to act a play on Saturday.'

She leant forward and regarded me with apprehension.

'But why not? I'll promise to clap.'

'You can't, because, you see, you're going to act too. Isn't it jolly?' said Myra breathlessly.

I gave what, if I hadn't just begun the last sweet, would have been a scornful laugh.

'Me act? Why, I've never—I don't do it—it isn't done—I don't act—not on Saturdays. How absurd!'

'Have you told him, Myra?' Dahlia called out suddenly.

'I'm telling him now. I think he's taking it all right.'

'Don't talk about me as "him"!' I said angrily. 'And I'm *not* taking it all right. I'm not taking it at all.'

'It's only such a very small part—we're all doing something, you know. And your costume's ordered and everything. But how awfully sporting of you.'

After that, what could I say?

'Er—what am I?' I asked modestly.

'You're a—a small rat-catcher,' said Myra cheerfully.

'I beg your pardon?'

'A rat-catcher.'

'You said a small one. Does that mean that I'm of diminu-
tive size, or that I'm in a small way of business, or that my
special line is young ones?'

'It means that you haven't much to say.'

'I see. And would you call it a tragic or a pathetic part?'

'It's a comic part, rather. You're Hereditary Rat-Catcher
to the Emperor Bong, Bong the Second. Not the first Bong,
the Dinner Bong.'

'Look here. I suppose you know that I've never acted in
my life, and never been or seen a rat-catcher in my life. It
is therefore useless for you to tell me to be perfectly natural.'

'You have so little to do; it will be quite easy. Your great
scene is where you approach the Emperor very nervously—'

'I shall do the nervous part all right.'

'And beg him to spare the life of his mother-in-law.'

'Why? I mean, who is she?'

'Miss Fortescue.'

'Yes, I doubt if I can make that bit seem quite so natural.
Still, I'll try.'

'Hooray. How splendid!'

'A rat-catcher,' I murmured to myself. 'Where is the rat?
The rat is on the mat. The cat is on the rat. The bat is on
the cat. The—'

'Mr Derry will go through your part with you tomorrow. Some of it is funnier than that.'

'The electrical engineer? What do they know about rat-
catching?'

'Nothing, only—'

'Aha! Now I see who your mysterious Mr Derry is. He is going to coach us.'

'He is. You've found it out at last. How bright green sweets make you.'

'They have to be really bright green sweets. Poor man! What a job he'll have with us all.'

'Yes,' said Myra, as she prepared to leave me. 'Now you know why he doesn't get up till ten.'

'In the rat-catching business,' I said thoughtfully, as I opened the door, 'the real rush comes in the afternoon. Rat-catchers, in consequence, never get up till ten-thirty. Do you know,' I decided, 'I am quite beginning to like my little part.'

9

The play was a great success; I know, because many of the audience told me so afterwards. Had they but guessed what was going on behind the scenes, the congratulations would have been even more enthusiastic. For as near as a touch we had to drop the eggproof curtain and hand the money back.

I am going to give you the opening scene as it was actually said—not as it was heard across the footlights—and then you will understand. The RAT-CATCHER (Me) and the MAID (Myra) take the stage first, and they introduce themselves in the usual way to the audience and each other. The scene is the palace of the EMPEROR BONG (Simpson). Very well then.

MAID (*sweetly*). Truly his Majesty is a handsome man, and I wonder not that his people love him.

RAT-CATCHER (*rather nervous*). Thou surprisest me. I saw him in the wings – in the winter garden just now—that is to say, anon—and thought him plain. But hush, here he comes.

(*They salaam, or whatever you call it, and stay there.*)

RAT-CATCHER (*still salaaming*). What's the silly ass waiting for? I can't stick this much longer; the blood's all going to my head like anything.

MAID (*in a similar position*). He must have forgotten his cue. Can't you say, 'Hush, here he comes,' again?

RAT-CATCHER. I can't say anything out loud in this position. Do you think I might come up for a breath?

MAID (*loudly*). His Majesty tarries.

RAT-CATCHER (*sotto voce*). He does. You've got it.

MAID. Whatever shall we do? Do think of something.

RAT-CATCHER. Well, I'm going to rise to the surface. I'm tired of being a submarine. (*They both stand up.*)

MAID (*brilliantly*). Perchance it was a rat we heard and not his Majesty.

RAT-CATCHER (*with equal brilliance*). Fear not, fair damsel. Behold, I will investigate. (*Proceeds to back of stage.*)

ARCHIE (*from wings*). Come off, you idiot.

RAT-CATCHER (*always the gentleman—to* MAID). Tarry a while, my heart, what time I seek assistance. (*Exit.*)

MAID (*confidentially to audience—to keep the thing going*). Truly he is a noble youth, though he follows a lowly profession. 'Tis not the apparel that proclaims the man. Methinks. . . .

ME (*annoyed*). Who's an idiot?

ARCHIE. Didn't you see me wink? That ass Simpson's banged his nose against a door-post and is bleeding like a pig. Says it's because he hadn't got his spectacles.

ME (*still annoyed*). More likely the champagne.

ARCHIE. They're dropping keys down his back as hard as they can. Will you and Myra gag a bit, till he's ready?

ME (*excitedly*). My good fool, how on earth—

MYRA (*coming to back of stage*). But behold he returns. (*Frowns imperiously.*)

RAT-CATCHER (*coming on again very unwillingly*). Ah, fair maid, 'tis thee. I bring thee good tidings. I met one in the anteroom, a long-legged, scurvy fellow, who did tell me that his Majesty was delayed on some business.

MAID. That must have been his Conjurer—I know him well. (*Aside.*) What's happened?

RAT-CATCHER. Let us then rest a while, an it please thee.

(*Seizing her by the arm.*) Over here. That ass Simpson's hurt himself. We've got to amuse the audience till he's finished bleeding.

MAID (*sitting down with her back to audience*). I say, is it really serious?

RAT-CATCHER. Not for him; it is for us. Now then, talk away.

MAID. Er—h'm. (*Coyly*). Wilt not tell me of thy early life, noble sir, how thou didst become a catcher of rats?

RAT-CATCHER (*disgusted*). You coward! (*Aloud.*) Nay, rather let me hear of thine own life. (*Aside.*) Scored.

MAID. That's not fair. I asked you first. (*Modestly.*) But I am such a little thing, and you are so noble a youth.

RAT-CATCHER. True. (*Having a dash at it.*) 'Twas thus. My father, when I was yet a child, didst—did—no, didst—apprentice me to a salad binger—

MAID (*with interest*). How dost one bing salads?

RAT-CATCHER (*curtly*). Ballad singer. And I would frequent the market place at noon, singing catches and glees, and receiving from the entranced populace divers coins, curses, bricks and other ornaments. One morn, as I was embarked upon a lovely ballad, '*Place me amidst the young gazelles,*' I was seized right suddenly from behind. (*Bored to death.*) I'm sick of this. We're supposed to be amusing the audience.

MAID. Oh, go on. I'm getting awfully amused.

EMPEROR (*audibly from green-room*). Confound it, it's begun again.

EXECUTIONER (*bitterly*). And to think that I spent *hours* putting red ink on my axe!

MAID (*with great presence of mind*). What's that? Surely *that* was a rat.

RAT-CATCHER (*greatly relieved*). It was. (*Getting up.*) Let's have Archie on, and see if he can amuse them a bit more. (*Aloud.*) I must finish my tale anon. Stay here, sweet child, what time I fetch my trusty terrier. (*Exit.*)

MAID. 'Tis a strange story he tells. How different from my own simple life. Born of proud but morbid parents. . . .

ARCHIE. What's up? Stick to it.

ME. Have you got such a thing as a trusty terrier on you?

ARCHIE (*feeling up his sleeve*). No.

ME. Well, the audience will be extremely disappointed if I don't bring one back. I practically promised them I would. Look here, why don't you come on and help? Everybody is getting horribly bored with us.

ARCHIE (*delightedly*). Oh, all right.

Enter RAT-CATCHER *and* CONJURER.

MAID. But behold, he returns *again*!

RAT-CATCHER (*excitedly*). Great news, fair lady, which this long-legged, scurvy fellow I told you of will impart to us.

MAID. Why, 'tis the Conjurer. Have you news for us, sir?

CONJURER (*with no illusions about the Oriental style*). Absolutely stop press. What is it you want to know? Racing? The Bong Selling Plate was won by Proboscis, McSimp up. Immense enthusiasm. Bank rate unchanged—quite right this cold weather. Excuse me a moment, sir, your moustache is coming off. No, the left wing—allow me to lend you a postage stamp. Do you prefer red or green?

MAID (*biting her lip*). Will you not give us news of the Emperor?

CONJURER. I will. His Majesty has met with a severe accident whilst out hunting this morning, being bitten by a buffalo.

MAID. Alas, what will my mistress say?

CONJURER. She has already said everything that was necessary. Her actual words were: 'Just like Bong.'

RAT-CATCHER (*seizing the opportunity*). His Majesty ordered me to meet him here at noon. Methinks I had better withdraw and return anon. (*Makes off hurriedly.*)

CONJURER (*seizing him*). Not so. He bade me command you to stay and sing to us. (*Sensation.*)

RAT-CATCHER (*huskily*). Alas, I have forgotten my voice— that is, I have left my music at home. I will go and fetch it. (*Has another dash.*)

CONJURER. Stay! Listen! (*They all listen.*)

SIMPSON (*in wings*). Thanks, thanks, that will be all right now. Oh no, quite, thanks. Oh, is this your key? Thanks, thanks. No, it doesn't matter about the other ones, they don't feel at all uncomfortable, thanks. Yes, I think it really did stop it, thanks.

CONJURER. I'm off! (*Aloud.*) His Majesty has regained consciousness. (*Exit.*)

SIMPSON (*apologetically*). Oh, Archie, I've got the billiard-room key in my—

RAT-CATCHER (*very loudly to* MAID). Hush, here he comes! (*They salaam.*)

(*Enter the* EMPEROR BONG.)

10

'Ladies and gentlemen,' said Simpson at the supper-table, glass in hand, 'it is my pleasant duty—'

'Bother!' murmured Myra. 'Drinking healths always makes me feel funny.'

'Silence for McSimp,' shouted Archie. 'Now then, pass along there, please. There's no need to push, you'll all be able to hear. Gentlemen, the O'Sumph is addressing us impromptu, not to say unasked.'

'It is my pleasant duty,' continued Simpson, 'as your late Emperor (*Half-an-hour-late. How's the probosc?*), to propose the health of the Rabbits Dramatic Company. (*Hooray!*) Great as we are on the cricket field (*Wide!*)—great, I say, as we are on the cricket field (*Pitch 'em up, Simpson*), we are, I think, still greater in the halls of Thespis. (*Don't know the lady.*) Gentlemen, I knew Irving. (*Liar!*) I have heard tell of Garrick (*Good! Ever heard of Shakespeare?*), but tonight has been a new experience for me. (*I will—give you—the kee—eys of—.*) Ladies and gentlemen, I propose our very good healths, coupled with the name of our hostess Miss Mannering.' (*Loud cheers.*).

'That's me,' said Myra.

'I single out Miss Mannering,' added Simpson, 'because I'm sure we should all like to hear her make a speech.'

'Oh, Samuel,' said Myra, shaking her head at him, 'and I thought it was because you loved me.'

'The Rabbits! Myra!' we cried.

'Miss Mannering will now address you,' announced Archie. 'She will be glad to answer any questions afterwards; but any one who interrupts will be hurled out. I appeal to you, as Englishmen, to give her a fair hearing.'

Myra stood on a chair, looking lovely, but very lonely, and waited till we were silent.

'My dear good friends,' she began, and then she caught Thomas's eye. 'Hallo, Tommy,' she said wistfully. . . . 'My dear good friends, but why should you say *I'm* a jolly good fellow, when it isn't my birthday or anything? But how *silly* of you! Why, of course, we're *all* jolly good fellows—and jolly good actors too. It *has* been fun, hasn't it? . . . Oh, Archie, dear. . . . I hope we shall all be here in the summer, don't you? Well, you can't very well say you don't, now I've asked you, can you? You'll have to pretend your uncles are very ill, and then you needn't come. . . . Oh, *please—don't* look at me like that, make me want to cry, and I only want to laugh tonight. . . . Archie, may I get down?'

'She *is* a dear,' Dahlia whispered to me. 'How you can go on—'

It was Simpson who saved the situation and made us merry and bright again. He hastily trotted out the suggestion that we should tour the country in the summer, playing cricket in the day and *Bong the Second* at night. Archie backed him up at once.

'Only I'm off Bong Two altogether,' he said. 'Of course, what we want is a cricket play. We shall have to write one ourselves, I expect; there aren't any really good ones about. Act I, Rupert Vavasour, a dashing bat and the last descendant of an ancient but impoverished house, is in love with the beautiful but equally impoverished Millicent. Milly is being pursued by a rich villain of the name of Jasper Fordyce, the said Jasper being a bowler of extreme swiftness, with a qualification for Essex. . . . Go on, Simpson.'

'In order to restore the fallen fortunes of the house, Rupert plays for Kent as a professional—Binks (R.)—and secures talent money in six successive matches. Jasper hears of it, and (Act II) assassinates the scorer, bribing a hireling of his own to take the deceased's place. In the next match Rupert only scores forty-nine.'

'Rupert,' continued Thomas, 'who had been counting his own jolly score, and made it eighty-seven, was furious, and determined at all costs to foil the villain. Accordingly he went on to bowl in the next innings and took five wickets for 239, thus obtaining talent money.'

'A little love interest, please, Dahlia,' said Archie.

'Now the captain, who was in the secret,' said Dahlia, 'was in love with Rupert's sister, which was why he put Binks (R.) on to bowl. As soon as Binks had collected his five wickets, Blythe went on, and took the other five for three runs. In this way Kent just managed to win, and so Rupert got more talent money.'

'The next match was against Essex—Act III the great act of the play—and Jasper Fordyce was playing for the Leyton brigade. As he put on his spurs before taking the field, and brushed his sleek black hair, he smiled sardonically to himself. Had he not overnight dug holes in the pitch at the pavilion end, and was not the wicket fiery, and he notoriously an erratic bowler?'

'Everything points to Simpson playing Jasper,' I said, and continued:

' "Heads," cried Jasper. It was heads. "I put you in" he remarked calmly. "What!" said the other in amazement. Ten minutes later Binks (R.) and Humphreys were at the wicket. Binks took first ball with a touch of nervousness at his heart. All depended on this match. If only he could make 450 to-day, he would be able to pay off the mortgage and marry his Millicent. . . . "Play." Jasper rushed up to the wicket and delivered the ball. Then before anybody could see how it happened, Rupert was stretched full-length upon the sward!'

'I had rather thought of playing Rupert myself,' said Archie. 'But I'm not so sure now.'

'Five for 239,' I reminded him. 'The part was written for you.'

'But what of Millicent?' said Myra. 'Fearing lest some evil should overtake her lover she had attended the match clad in a long ulster, and now she flung this off, revealing the fact that she was in flannels. With her hair tucked up beneath her county cap she looked a slim and handsome boy. To rush on to the field and take the injured one's place was the work of the moment. "Who is this?" said the umpires in amazement. "Fear not," whispered Millicent to Humphreys, "I have a birth qualification for the county, and the gardener coached me for an hour last night." '

'Once more Jasper rushed up to the crease, and the spectators held their breath.'

'I'm going to be a spectator,' I said, 'with a breath-holding part. Sorry—go on, Blair.'

'Then Millicent's bat flashed, and behold! the ball was on the boundary! A torrent of cheers rent the air. Again he bowled, again the bat flashed. Jasper ground his teeth.

'The curtain goes down here to represent the passing of an hour. When it rises again, Millicent's score is 423. There was dead silence for a moment. Then Millicent swung her bat. And at that the cheers broke out, such cheering as had never been heard before. Maclaren's record score was beaten at last! "Now surely he will knock his wickets down," said the spectators. Little did they know that until 450 was upon the tins the mortgage could not be paid off! Four hundred and thirty—440—449—a sharply run single—450! From the pavilion Rupert heard the cheers and fainted again.

'It was "over", and Millicent had the bowling. Jasper delivered the ball, a fast half-volley—'

('Oh, Simpson simply *must* play Jasper.')

'—and Millicent drove it back hard and true. Jasper tried to duck, but it was too late. He was dead.

'Act IV. All his money went to Rupert, who was a distant cousin. He married Millicent, and they lived happily ever after. But, though they are always to be seen at the Tonbridge and Canterbury weeks, they have never played cricket again. *Curtain.*'

'And bedtime,' said Myra suddenly. 'Good-night, everybody.'

Batter Sweet: or 'Not Cricket'

An Operetta by A. P. HERBERT

To follow A. A. Milne's play, here is a suggested comic opera by his fellow Punch *contributor Sir Alan Herbert. 'A. P.' was, by all accounts, a cunning slow bowler—'in the style afterwards adopted by Laker and Lock,' he joked—and once while he was an M.P. he played for the House of Commons against the Lords and took five wickets. On another fondly remembered occasion, when batting for an Authors' XI—which included Nigel Balchin, Cecil Day Lewis and A. G. Macdonell—he scored fifty-three and hit a six right over a sight-screen!*

In a number of his essays and stories Sir Alan could not resist poking fun at those who viewed cricket as something little short of a religion. 'I cannot accept,' he once wrote, 'that it is the nurse of noble character and the school for saints. It is a tough and terrible, rough, unscrupulous and ruthless game.' He was perhaps being a bit tongue-in-cheek, but 'A. P.' would certainly be an ideal man to have around if things got a bit too serious in any match. The gentle sarcasm of which this master of comedy was capable is very evident in the unusual contribution which follows.

Music by Vivian Ellis

(With respectful compliments to Mr Noel Coward, who has surprisingly neglected the National Game.)

Prologue

Front-cloth, a nursery. An elderly lady, strikingly beautiful in spite of her advanced years and white hair, is wheeled on L. in a bathchair.
A small boy bounds on R. carrying a small cricket-bat.

MAX. Oh, Granny, may I play with this bat?

LADY BANE (*gently*). Mais, mon petit, c'est le 'bat' de Grand'-mère. Where did you find it?

MAX. In your secret cupboard, Granny. (*smelling the bat*) It smells of lavender.

LADY BANE. You know you mustn't play with Granny's toys.

MAX (*stoutly*). But, Granny, when I grow up I'm going to be a soldier and kill the Australians.

[*He makes a violent gesture with the bat, as if bringing it
down upon the head of an enemy.*

LADY BANE *is much moved and sobs quietly.*]

MAX. Oh, Granny, what is it?

LADY BANE (*sings*). La vie est dure
                         Un peu d'amour—
                         Et puis bonjour.
                         (*Music*)

MAX (*clinging to knee,* L.):
           Granny, tell me, Granny, have you
               anything upon your mind?
           I'll give you a penny.
           Let me tenderly partake
           Of your evident heartache—
               Will you tell me the tale?

           Can it be some poignant recollection
               has revived an old affection?
           Can it be that this little toy
           Has awakened the brittle joy
               Of a dream that is stale?

LADY BANE. Ah—ah!

MAX. Does it bring back again
           The ecstasy and subtle pain
               Of yesterday?

LADY BANE. C'est vrai.
               (*frantic with reminiscence*)
           Fling away—all fettering things,
           Find a way—of bettering things;
               Shatter whatever
               Spoils our endeavour
           To keep our love gallant and gay.
           Let us dream—romantical things,
           Though they seem—impractical things;
               Let romance lead you
                   On, for I need you.

>   If things impede you
>   Fling them far away.

Scene I

SCENE: *Lord's Cricket Ground on the occasion of the Oxton and
Camrow Match. A sunny day.*
Time: The present—and the end of the luncheon interval.

The Parade
(*Music*)

FIRST SPECTATOR. The wicket's wearing.
SECOND SPECTATOR. And how is Madge?
THIRD SPECTATOR. The bowling's putrid.
FOURTH SPECTATOR. What batting!
FIFTH SPECTATOR. Have a good lunch?
SIXTH SPECTATOR. They can't play forward nowadays.
Enter three YOUNG CRICKETERS, *arm-in-arm. Flannels, blue
blazers, caps, and scarves and long cigarette-holders. Each car-
ries, or rather dangles, a bat.*

      *A bell rings and a policeman begins to clear the ground.
The crowd melt away gradually.*]

>   Sprigs of nobility we,
>   Twigs on the Family Tree.
>   Like every one else in the plays of dear
>   Howard
>   We're flowers that wonder just why we
>   have flowered—
>   Delicate cuttings of class,
>   Why are we kept under glass?
>   Life's such a bore—
>   What are we for?
>   Sprigs of nobility we—we—we, sprigs of
>   nobility we!

>   At our most expensive schools the
>   masters taught the rules

Of cricket, football, squash—in fact,
    of all games,
And sent us up to college with the
    satisfying knowledge
That life is just another of the
    ball games.
    If a boy can keep his bat
    Perpendicular (like that),
He is sure to be successful as a
    banker;

    If he's handy in the slips
    He is certain to eclipse
The business-man whose game is
    Crown and Anchor.
In every trade and calling take the
    richest and the greatest—
Their brains may be appalling, but
    their bats, you'll find, were
    straightest;
    While huddle in the jails
    Or on the gallows dangle
The miserable males
    Whose bats were at an angle,
And those who dropped a sitter
    Or played forward to half-volleys
In squalor long and bitter
    Must expiate their follies.

    Sprigs of nobility we,
    Twigs on the Family Tree,
We've wielded this curious weapon
    correctly
And so we may count on an income
    directly;
    Possibly, probably shove
    Into His Majesty's Gov.;
    Still, we implore:

What are we for?
Sprigs of nobility we—we—we, sprigs of
nobility we!

[*Exeunt* R. *the* YOUNG MEN. *Enter* R. (*higher up*) *two*
UMPIRES *in white coats, carrying enormous books labelled
'The Laws of Cricket'. One should be tall, one short and
round; both, if possible, basses. They enter pompously to
Handelian music.*]

BOTH. We are the British Umpire,
      Of Equity the model,
   And the hearts of our race beat twice
        the pace
      As to the pitch we waddle.
FIRST U. These are the Laws,
SECOND U. . . . do. . . .
First U. . . . do. . . .
SECOND U. . . . do. . . .
FIRST U. These are the Rules,
      The cause of fear
SECOND U. To knaves or fools
      Who flout 'em.
FIRST U. But we have heard
      They're not quite clear,
SECOND U. And so a word
BOTH.   About 'em.
FIRST U. Few men can say—
SECOND U.   Not I, for one—
FIRST U. What is or is not cricket;
SECOND U. But, briefly, anything may be done,
FIRST U. So long as the other side stick it.
      The bowlers may strike batsmen down.
      With hideous blows on trunk or crown;
SECOND U. A captain may compel the foe
      To bat in darkness, fog or snow;
FIRST U. And if the foe does not protest

SECOND U. We take it all is for the best.
FIRST U. All dirty tricks shall we allow,
SECOND U. Provided no one makes a row
           Or dies upon the wicket.
FIRST U. But if a player starts a jaw,
SECOND U. That player has infringed the law,
           In short, it is not cricket—
FIRST U. Not cricket—
SECOND U. Not cricket—
BOTH.   Not cri-i-i-ck—
       —Not cri-i-i-ck—   (*ad lib.*)
   In short, it is not cricket.

[*Both turn and march up-stage to their posts, one going off* R.
    *The Camrow team come out on to the field to take their
    places.*]

BALLET

[*Loud applause as* HOWARD *and* SECOND BATSMAN
emerge from the Pavilion (R.) *and proceed towards the
wicket.* HOWARD *touches his dark-blue cap and hitches up
his trousers. His bat is a veteran bound with many strap-
pings, and is a tawny brown. He is a tenor—dark and
sinister.*

    SADIE *runs forward and confronts him. She carries under
her arm a small, new, very white-looking bat.* SECOND
BATSMAN *goes on and off—up-left.*

    BASIL, *the Camrow captain, 'clean-limbed' and athletic,
stands down left, ready to field, and listens grimly to this
scene.*]

HOWARD (*halting*). You!
SADIE. Howard, I hear you are captain of Oxton now.
HOWARD. Yes. Isn't it foul?
SADIE. Isn't it rather big to be at the top of the tree?
HOWARD (*with a bitter little laugh*). It's a lonely place, Sadie,

the top of the tree. There's nothing up there but last year's birds'-nests.

SADIE. You're so unserious.

[*With sudden passion he kisses her.* BASIL *observes the gesture with dissatisfaction.*]

HOWARD (*breaking away*). How beastly! Sadie, we shall have to marry. Do you mind?

SADIE. I should hate it. (*intense*) Howard, let's get away from our horrible set—away to the South, to the sunshine.

HOWARD. To escape from our horrible set you'll have to go North. The South is crawling with it.

SADIE. Nobody but you could make cricket decadent. And yet—I hate it too. Will you make a hundred today?

HOWARD (*shaking his head*). Running wearies me. Besides, a century's so snobbish.

SADIE (*a sudden decision*). Howard, if you make a hundred I'll marry you.

HOWARD. And if I make nought you'll live with me. Is that it?

SADIE. I want to see if you can do something *big*. (*holding out her bat*) I have bought you a bat.

HOWARD. I have a bat.

SADIE (*looks at his bat with disgust*). But it's strapped up like a duchess. Use my little clean bat, Howard.

HOWARD (*looking at her*). My dear, a virgin bat is no more use than a virgin cow.

SADIE. Oh, Howard! (*pressing him*) To please me!

HOWARD. Angel, I can't carry two bats.

SADIE. Why not? The tennis-champions carry six.

HOWARD. But they play with six balls. (*yielding, puts her bat under his arm*) Very well, fish-face.

[*He is going to embrace her but she stops him.*]

SADIE (*looking down at his pads and fingering his gloves*). Darling, I don't think you ought to kiss me in those things. It's *too* inelegant.

HOWARD. Darling, how right you are! Off with them!

[*She kneels and unbuckles his pads while he takes off his gloves.*]

SADIE *and* HOWARD:
      Fling away—all fettering things!
      Find a way—of bettering things.
         Shatter whatever
         Spoils our endeavour
           To keep our love gallant and gay!
      Let us dream—romantical things,
      Though they seem—impractical things;
         Let romance lead you
         On, for I need you!
         If pads impede you
           Fling them far away!

Terrific musical climax. SADIE *and* HOWARD *vehemently fling one pad away each, one of them being caught, in self-defence and indignantly, by* BASIL, *who throws it off into the wings.*
    HOWARD *then kisses* SADIE *and marches up-stage to the wicket.*
                (Music)
    SADIE *goes towards her seat, down-left, but on the way she and* BASIL *suddenly see each other. They stop and stare, registering intensity.*]

SADIE (*glances up-stage, then back to* BASIL, *dazed*). Hell! Have I made a mistake? (*passes on, still dazed, to her seat, down-left*)

[*Meanwhile* HOWARD *is taking 'guard', etc. The score-board is illuminated and gives the following information:*
    *Batsman—*HOWARD
    Score—
    *Bowler—*ENDIVE
    *Father's name—*LORD FENNEL

Clubs—CARLTON *and* BUCK'S

HOWARD *flourishes his bat, there is a sharp crack, field-ers relax and* HOWARD'S *score at once leaps up to '10'.*

During the following the game proceeds quietly at the back, HOWARD'S *score leaping up by tens and fifteens.*

Enter, down-left, three LADIES OF LORDS.]

FIRST L.L. (*without looking towards the field, hearing the applause*). Oh, my dear, has something happened?

SECOND L.L. My dear, what *could* happen? They seem to do *nothing* but drink lemonade.

THIRD L.L. It's *too* stupefying.

FIRST L.L. And yet the *moment* one relaxes somebody gets out or something and one misses the *real* event of the season.

SECOND L.L. Oh, *darling*—there's *Basil*! (*calling to the Camrow captain*) '*Basil* darling!'

[BASIL *turns and, self-conscious, motions them with his hand to be quiet.*]

SECOND L.L. Oh, *darling*, don't be *pedantic*! I *only* wanted a *cigarette*!

[*All, yawning, turn front.*]

All three.   Ladies of Lord's,
                    Easily-boreds,
        And frantic from sitting like sardines
                    Sucking hot sweets
                    And ignoring the feats
        Of our embryo Hobbses and Jardines,
                    Ladies of Lord's,
                    Oh, how we suffer,
                    Sitting on boards
                    And growing no tougher!
        We don't understand what it's all about—
        Why do they keep throwing that ball about?
        Every half-hour they have drinks taken out,
        But nobody'd care if we *died* of the drought.
                    Ladies of Lord's!

> It's treason to state it,
> But, oh, how we hate it,
> The Ladies of Lord's!

> Ladies of Lord's,
> Mortally-boreds!
It's all very well for our brothers.
> Maybe it's fun
> To run round in the sun;
They don't have to sit next to their mothers.
> Nobody cares,
> It's all very tiring;
> Every one stares
> At young men perspiring.
It's a game that develops the character
(As the schoolmistress said when they
> barracked her),
But, though it is good for our brothers, no
> doubt,
It seems to bring all that is worst in us out!
> Ladies of Lord's!
> It's treason to state it,
> But, oh, how we hate it,
> The Ladies of Lord's!
> [LADIES OF LORD'S *exeunt*—R.

A waiter brings on to the field from the pavilion a tray full of glasses, with a jug of lemonade. The players bound towards him and pose with glasses round him.

During this, SADIE (*who has formed a passion for the handsome* BASIL) *goes to him.*]

SADIE. Are you really Basil Mayhew?

BASIL. Yes.

SADIE (*intense*). I might have known.

BASIL. Tell me, is it true that you will marry him if he makes a hundred?

SADIE. It was. Do you think he will?

BASIL (*grimly*). Not if I know it! His late-cuts poison the air!

SADIE. Oh, Basil, since I have watched you in the long-field I have understood cricket at last. (*holding out the bat*) Will you teach me?

THE CRICKET LESSON

[SADIE *makes passes with her bat;* BASIL, *gesturing with an imaginary bat, shows her what to do.*]

BASIL. No, Miss Sadie, that's unsound;
    Bring that left elbow more round!
        No, not like that!
        Excellent! you have it pat.

[SADIE, *miraculously, knows the whole art already.*]

    All our lives we will be two good cricketers
        In our cosy little flat,
    Pillars of the Church and season-ticketers,
        Joined together by a bat.
SADIE (*speaks*). When may I bowl some one, please?
BASIL. Not until you are confirmed and have a permit from the Foreign Office.
SADIE (*sings*). Something so deep in my soul
        Tells me that I'd like to bowl.
           (*Waltz*)
    I'll play games with you
    Whenever you've no dames with you;
        You'll be the bat—I the ball,
        And you can hit me anywhere at all.

    Then I'll bowl to you,
    Surrender my whole soul to you—
        All the common world will seem
        Players in a distant dream—
        You and I will be a team
           Of two.

[HOWARD, *up-stage, observes the end of this affecting scene with dismay, but the Lemonade Interval is over, the fielders return to their places, and* HOWARD, *with a long lingering look, goes back to the wicket, i.e.* OFF, *up* R.

The players (and SADIE*) return to their places.*

HOWARD'S *score is now eighty-two.*

There has been an over, and HOWARD *is now batting* OFF, *i.e.* R. *We therefore see the* SECOND BATSMAN *and the* UMPIRE; *and we now see the* BOWLER *run on from* L., *bound into the air and fling the ball into the wings. There is a crack, applause, and* HOWARD'S *score leaps up to ninety-nine.*]

SPECTATORS (*in unison*). Ninety-nine!

[BASIL, *now down-left, is in a fever of tension. All lean forward eagerly.*

(*Chord*)

The BOWLER *bowls, there is a crack, the* SECOND BATSMAN *runs off, and* HOWARD *runs on; but he halts and, like every one else, gazes skyward. He has struck the ball very high into the air and it looks like falling in* BASIL'S *neighbourhood.* BASIL *shows that he is aware of this by dodging anxiously about.*]

(*Music*)

MELODRAMA

As the ball approaches—

BASIL.   See the ball!
            It must fall.
      Clinging fingers, play your part!
            Happiness is near
         If you grip—grip it with a will:
            It may disappear
      Like the whip-whippoor-whippoor-will.

[*The ball comes into view, descending slowly at the end of a string.*]

SADIE (*rising*)   Give romance
Every chance—
Catch it bravely, though it smart.
Tra-la-la-la, *etc.*

Both.   Love is all!
Hold the ball,

And you hold $\begin{Bmatrix} my \\ her \end{Bmatrix}$ heart.

[*The ball halts in mid-air.* BASIL *and* SADIE *turn front and sing to the audience, supported by all the Lord's audience and players:*

See the ball! *etc.*

Finally BASIL *turns up-stage, the ball descends and he catches it. Applause. Sensation.*]

FINALE

But HOWARD, *who all this time has been running runs, now bounds down-stage and, gracefully, elegantly, but none the less forcibly, strikes* BASIL *on the head with the little white bat.*

BASIL *falls to the ground and lies on his side, facing the footlights, dead, but holding up, tightly clasped against his chest, the fatal ball.*

SADIE *runs to him and kneels at his side.*

The CROWD *cluster behind.*

TABLEAU

But the picture is broken up by the UMPIRE *(bowler's end), who thrusts his way through the crowd (centre) and inspects the body (or rather the ball—the only thing that interests him). Assured that the ball has not touched the ground, he rises to his full height, points a majestic finger to heaven and says in a great voice—*

'OUT!'

(*Very loud music*)

FULL COMPANY

Fling away—all fettering things, *etc.*

CURTAIN

How's That, Umpire?

by P. G. WODEHOUSE

The great 'Plum' Wodehouse would have to be a member of the team, not only because of his undoubted skill at cricket but also because no anthology of humour would be complete without one of his masterpieces. Wodehouse's lifelong interest in the game started when he was at Dulwich College, where he opened the bowling, and continued as a member of the Authors' XI in company with Sir Arthur Conan Doyle, Reginald Berkeley and Clifford Bax. Playing against a Publishers' XI one year, he considerably enhanced his cricketing reputation—though perhaps dented his publishing prospects a little – by clean bowling four of London's leading publishers and then scoring an unbeaten sixty!

Wodehouse's interest in the game is evident in his work: vide *the exploits of his 'cricketing genius' Mike Jackson (in* Mike at Wrykyn *and* Mike and Psmith, *both 1953) which were inspired by his days at Dulwich; and, of course, the immortal Jeeves was named after one of his heroes, the Warwickshire fast bowler, Percy Jeeves. His devotion to the game did not make him blind to its funnier side, though, and some of his earliest contributions to* Punch *make gentle fun of the game. Among his numerous short stories in which cricket features, 'How's That, Umpire?', which he wrote in 1950, is perhaps less well-known than some and certainly ideally suited to this collection.*

THE story of Conky Biddle's great love begins at about six-forty-five on an evening in June in the Marylebone district of London. He had spent the day at Lord's cricket ground watching a cricket match, and driving away at close of play had been held up in a traffic jam. And held up alongside his taxi was a car with a girl at the wheel. And he had just lit a cigarette and was thinking of this and that, when he heard her say:

'Cricket is not a game. It is a mere shallow excuse for walking in your sleep.'

It was at this point that love wound its silken fetters about Conky. He leaped like a jumping bean and the cigarette fell from his nerveless fingers. If a girl who talked like that was not his dream girl, he didn't know a dream girl when he heard one.

You couldn't exactly say that he fell in love at first sight, for owing to the fact that in between him and her, obscuring the visibility, there was sitting a robust blighter in blue flannel with a pin stripe, he couldn't see her. All he had to go on was her voice, but that was ample. It was a charming

175

voice with an American intonation. She was probably, he thought, an American angel who had stepped down from Heaven for a short breather in London.

'If I see another cricket game five thousand years from now,' she said, 'that'll be soon enough.'

Her companion plainly disapproved of these cracks. He said in a stiff, sniffy sort of way that she had not seen cricket at its best that afternoon, play having been greatly interfered with by rain.

'A merciful dispensation,' said the girl. 'Cricket with hardly any cricket going on is a lot better than cricket where the nuisance persists uninterrupted. In my opinion the ideal contest would be one where it rained all day and the rival teams stayed home doing their crossword puzzles.'

The traffic jam then broke up and the car shot forward like a B.29, leaving the taxi nowhere.

The reason why this girl's words had made so deep an impression on the young Biddle was that of all things in existence, with the possible exception of slugs and his uncle Everard, Lord Plumpton, he disliked cricket most. As a boy he had been compelled to play it, and grown to man's estate he was compelled to watch it. And if there was one spectacle that saddened him more than another in a world where the man of sensibility is always being saddened by spectacles, it was that of human beings, the heirs of the ages, waddling about in pads and shouting 'How's that, umpire?'

He had to watch cricket because Lord Plumpton told him to, and he was dependent on the other for his three squares a day. Lord Plumpton was a man who knew the batting averages of every first-class cricketer back to the days when they used to play in top hats and whiskers, and recited them to Conky after dinner. He liked to show Conky with the assistance of an apple (or, in winter, of an orange) how Bodger of Kent got the fingerspin which enabled him to make the ball dip and turn late on a sticky wicket. And frequently when Conky was walking along the street with him and working up to touching him for a tenner, he would break off the conversation at its most crucial point in order to demonstrate with his umbrella how Codger of Sussex made his late cut through the slips.

It was to the home of this outstanding louse, where he had a small bedroom on an upper floor, that Conky was now on his way. Arriving at journey's end, he found a good deal of stir and bustle going on, with doctors coming downstairs with black bags and parlourmaids going upstairs with basins of gruel, and learned from the butler that Lord Plumpton had sprained his ankle.

'No, really?' said Conky, well pleased, for if his uncle had possessed as many ankles as a centipede he would thoroughly have approved of him spraining them all. 'I suppose I had better go up and view the remains.'

He proceeded to the star bedroom and found his uncle propped up with pillows, throwing gruel at the parlourmaid. It was plain that he was in no elfin mood. He was looking like a mass murderer, though his face lacked the genial expression which you often see in mass murderers, and he glared at Conky with the sort of wild regret which sweeps over an irritable man when he sees a loved one approaching his sick bed and realises that he has used up all the gruel.

'What ho, Uncle Everard,' said Conky. 'The story going the round of the clubs is that you have bust a joint of sorts. What happened?'

Lord Plumpton scowled darkly. He looked now like a mass murderer whose stomach ulcers are paining him.

'I'll tell you what happened. You remember I had to leave you at Lord's to attend a committee meeting at my club. Well, as I was walking back from the club, there were some children playing cricket in the street and one of them skied the ball towards extra cover, so naturally I ran out into the road to catch it when a homicidal lunatic of a girl came blinding along at ninety miles an hour in her car and knocked me base over apex. One of these days,' said Lord Plumpton, licking his lips, 'I hope to meet that girl again, preferably down a dark alley. I shall skin her very slowly with a blunt knife, dip her in boiling oil, sever her limb from limb, assemble those limbs on the pavement and dance on them.'

'And rightly,' said Conky. 'These girls who bust your ankles and prevent you going to Lord's tomorrow need a sharp lesson.'

'What do you mean, prevent me going to Lord's tomorrow? Do you think a mere sprained ankle will stop me going to a cricket match? I shall be there, with you at my side. And now,' said Lord Plumpton, wearying of these exchanges, 'go to hell!'

Conky did not go to hell, but he went downstairs and out on the front steps to get a breath of air. He was feeling low and depressed. He had been so certain that he would be able to get tomorrow off. He had turned to go in again when he heard a noise of brakes as a car drew up behind him.

'Excuse me,' said a voice. 'Could I see Lord Plumpton?'

Simple words, but their effect on Conky as he recognised that silvery voice was to make him quiver from stay-combed hair to shoe sole. He uttered a whinnying cry which, as he swivelled round and for the first time was privileged to see her face, became a gasp. The voice had been the voice of an angel. The face measured up to the voice.

Seeing him, she too gasped. This was apt to be the reaction of the other sex on first beholding Conky Biddle, for though his I.Q. was low his outer crust was rather sensational. He was, indeed, a dazzlingly good-looking young man, who out-Caryed Grant and began where Gregory Peck left off.

'I say,' he said, going to the car and placing a foot on the running-board, 'Don't look now, but did I by chance hear you expressing a wish to meet my uncle, Lord Plumpton?'

'That's right. I recently flattened him out with my car, and I was planning to give him some flowers.'

'I wouldn't,' said Conky. 'I really wouldn't. I say this as a friend. Time, the great healer, will have to pull up its socks

and spit on its hands quite a bit before it becomes safe for
you to enter the presence.'

'I see. Then I'll take the blooms around the corner and have
them delivered by a messenger boy. How's that, umpire?'

Corky winced. It was as though he had heard this divine
creature sully her lips with something out of a modern historical novel.

'Good God!' he said. 'Where did you pick up that obscene
expression?'

'From your uncle. He was chanting it at the top of his
voice when I rammed him. A mental case, I imagine. What
does it mean?'

'It's what you say at cricket.'

'Cricket!' The girl shuddered strongly. 'Shall I tell you
what I think of cricket?'

'I have already heard your views. Your car got stuck abaft
my taxi in a traffic block this evening. I was here, if you
follow what I mean, and you were there, a few feet to the
nor'-nor'-east, so I was able to drink in what you were
saying about cricket. Would you mind if I thanked you with
tears in my eyes?'

'Not at all. But don't you like cricket? I thought all Englishmen loved it.'

'Not this Englishman. It gives me the pip.'

'Me, too. I ought never to have gone near that Lord's
place. But in a moment of weakness I let myself be talked
into it by my *fiancé*.'

Conky reeled.

'Oh, my sainted aunt! Have you got a *fiancé*?'

'Not now.'

Conky stopped reeling.

'Was he the bloke you were talking to in the car?'

'That's right. Eustace Davenport-Simms. I think he plays
for Essex or Sussex or somewhere. My views were too
subversive for him, so after kidding back and forth for a
while we decided to cancel the order for the wedding cake.'

'I thought he seemed a bit sniffy.'

'He got sniffier.'

'Very sensible of you not to marry a cricketer.'

'So I felt.'

'The upshot, then, when all the smoke has blown away, is that you are once more in circulation?

'Yes.'

'Well, that's fine,' said Conky. A sudden thought struck him. 'I say, would you object if I pressed your little hand?'

'Some other time, I think.'

'Any time that suits you.'

'You see, I have to hie me back to my hotel and dress. I'm late already, and my father screams like a famished hyæna if he's kept waiting for his rations.'

And with a rapid thrust of her shapely foot she set the machinery in motion and vanished round the corner on two wheels, leaving Conky staring after her with a growing feeling of desolation. He had just realised that he was unaware of her name, address and telephone number and had had what was probably his last glimpse of her. If the expression 'Ships that pass in the night' had been familiar to him, he would certainly have uttered it, using clenched teeth for the purpose.

It was a Conky with heart bowed down and a general feeling of having been passed through the wringer who accompanied his uncle to Lord's next morning. The thought that a Grade A soulmate had come into his life and buzzed out again, leaving no clue to her identity or whereabouts, was a singularly bitter one. Lord Plumpton on the journey to the Mecca of cricket spoke well and easily of the visit of the Australian team of 1921, but Conky proved a distrait listener; so distrait that Lord Plumpton prodded him irascibly in the ribs and called him an infernal goggle-eyed fathead, which of course he was.

He was still in a sort of trance when they took their seats in the pavilion, but here it was less noticeable, for everybody else was in a sort of trance. The somnambulists out in the field tottered to and fro, and the spectators lay back and let their eyes go glassy. For perhaps an hour nothing happened except that Hodger of Middlesex, waking like Abou ben Adhem from a deep dream of peace, flicked his bat at a rising ball and edged it into the hands of a sleeper dozing in what is technically known as the gully. Then Lord Plumpton, who had been silent except for an occasional 'Nice! Nice!' sat up with a sudden jerk and an explosive 'Well, I'm dashed!' and glared sideways at the three shilling seats which adjoined the pavilion. And Conky, following his gaze, felt his heart execute four separate buck and wing steps and come to rest quivering like a jelly in a high wind.

'Well, I'm dashed!' said Lord Plumpton, continuing to direct at the three shilling seats the kind of look usually associated with human fiends in mystery stories. 'There's that blasted girl!'

It was not a description which Conky himself would have applied to the divinest of her sex, nor one which he enjoyed hearing applied to her, and for a moment he was in two minds as to whether to haul off and sock his relative on the beezer. Wiser counsels prevailed, and he said:

'Yes, there she spouts.'

Lord Plumpton seemed surprised.

'You know her?'

'Just slightly. She ran into me last night.'

'Into you, too? Good gad, the female's a public menace. If she's allowed to remain at large, the population of London will be decimated. I've a good mind to go over and tell her what I think of her.'

'But your uncle, ankle.'

'What the devil are you gibbering about?'

'I mean your ankle, uncle. You mustn't walk about on it. How would it be if I popped over and acquainted her with your displeasure?'

Lord Plumpton considered.

'Yes, that's not a bad idea. A surprisingly good idea, in fact, considering what a nitwit you are. But pitch it strong.'

'Oh, I will,' said Conky.

He rose and hurried off, and Lord Plumpton fell into conversation with the barely animate spectator on his left. They were soon deep in an argument as to whether it was at square-leg or at extra-cover that D. C. L. Wodger of Gloucestershire had fielded in 1904.

If the girl had looked like the better class of angel in the uncertain light of last night, she looked more than ever so in the reasonably. bright sunshine of today. She was one of those lissom girls of medium height. Her eyes and hair were a browny hazel. The general effect was of a seraph who ate lots of yeast.

'Oh, hullo,' said Conky, lowering himself into a seat beside her. 'We meet again, what?'

She seemed surprised and startled. In her manner, as she gazed at his clean-cut face and then into his frank blue eyes, there was something that might almost be described as fluttering.

'You!' she cried. 'What are you doing here?'

'Just watching cricket.'

'But you told me last night that cricket gave you the pip, which I imagine is something roughly equivalent to the megrims or the heeby-jeebies.'

'Quite. But, you see, it's like this. My uncle is crazy about the ghastly game and I'm dependent on him, so when he says "Come along and watch cricket," I have to come along and watch it like a lynx.'

The girl frowned. It was as if she had been hurt and disappointed.

'Why are you dependent on your uncle? Why don't you get a job?'

Conky hastened to defend himself.

'I do get a job. I get dozens of jobs. But I lose them all. The trouble is, you see, that I'm not very bright.'

'No?'

'Not very. That's why they call me Conky.'

'Do they call you Conky?'

'Invariably. What started it was an observation one of the masters at school happened to drop one day. He said, addressing me—"To attempt to drive information into your head, Biddle, is no easy task, for Providence, mysterious in its workings, has given you instead of the more customary human brain a skull full of concrete." So after that everyone called me Conky.'

'I see. What sort of jobs have you tried?'

'Practically everything except Chancellor of the Duchy of Lancaster.'

'And you get fired every time?'

'Every time.'

'I'm sorry.'

'It's dashed white of you to be sorry, but as a matter of fact it's all right.'

'How do you mean it's all right?'

Conky hesitated. Then he reflected that if you couldn't confide in an angel in human shape, who could you confide in? He glanced about him. Except for themselves, the three shilling tier of seats was almost empty.

'Well, you'll keep it under your hat, won't you, because it's supposed to be very hush-hush at the moment. I am on the eve of making a stupendous fortune. You know sea water?'

'The stuff that props the ship up when you come over from New York?'

'That's right. Well, you probably aren't aware of it, but it's full of gold, and I'm in with a fellow who's got a secret process for scooping it out. I saw his advertisement in the paper saying that if you dashed along and brassed up quick you could get in on an invention of vast possibilities, so I dashed along and brassed up. He was a nice chap and let me into the thing without a murmur. Bloke of the name of MacSporran. I happened to have scraped up ten quid, so I put that in and he tells me that at a conservative estimate I shall get back about two hundred and fifty thousand. I call that a nice profit.'

'Very nice.'

'Yes, it's all very convenient. And when I say that, I'm not thinking so much of the jolliness of having all that splosh in the old sock, I am alluding more to the difference this has made in what you might call my matrimonial plans. If I want to get married, I mean. What I'm driving at', said Conky, giving her a melting look, 'is that I am now in a position, when I meet the girl I love, to put the binge on a practical basis.'

'I see.'

'In fact,' said Conky, edging a little closer, 'I might almost start making my plans at once.'

'That's the spirit. Father's slogan is "Do it now," and he's a tycoon.'

'I thought a tycoon was a sort of storm.'

'No, a millionaire.'

'Is your father a millionaire?'

'Yes, and more pouring in all the time.'

'Oh?'

A sudden chill had come over Conky's dashing mood. The one thing he had always vowed he would never do was marry for money. For years his six uncles and seven aunts had been urging him to cash in on his looks and grab something opulent. They had paraded heiresses before him in droves, but he had been firm. He had his principles.

Of course, in the present case it was different. He loved this girl with every fibre of his being. But all the same . . . No, he told himself, better wait till his bank balance was actually bulging.

With a strong effort he changed the conversation.

'Well, as I was saying,' he said, 'I hope to clean up shortly on an impressive scale, and when I do I'll never watch another cricket match as long as I live. Arising from which, what on earth are you doing here, holding the views on cricket which you do?'

A slight shadow of disappointment seemed to pass over the girl's face. It was as if she had been expecting the talk to develop along different lines.

'Oh, I came for a purpose.'

'Eh? What purpose?'

She directed his attention to the rows of living corpses in the pavilion. Lord Plumpton and his friend, having settled the Wodger question, were leaning back with their hats over their eyes. It was difficult to realise that life still animated those rigid limbs.

'When I was here yesterday, I was greatly struck by the spectacle of those stiffs over there. I wondered if it was possible to stir them up into some sort of activity.'

'I doubt it.'

'I'm a little dubious myself. They're like fish on a slab or a Wednesday matinee audience. Still, I thought I would try. Yesterday, of course I hadn't elastic and ammo with me.'

'Elastic? Ammo?'

Conky stared. From the recesses of her costume she had produced a piece of stout elastic and a wad of tin foil. She placed the tin foil on the elastic and then between her teeth. Then, turning, she took careful aim at Lord Plumpton.

For a sighting shot it was an admirable effort. Conky, following the projectile with a rapt gaze, saw his uncle start and put a hand to his ear. There seemed little reason to doubt that he had caught it amidships.

'Good Lord!' he cried. 'Here, after you with that elastic. I used to do that at school, and many was the fine head I secured. I wonder if the old skill still lingers.'

It was some minutes later that Lord Plumpton turned to the friend beside him.

'Wasps very plentiful this year,' he said.

The friend blinked drowsily.

'Watts?'

'Wasps.'

'There was A. R. K. Watts who used to play for Sussex. Ark we used to call him.'

'Not Watts. Wasps.'

'Wasps?'

'Wasps.'

'What about them?'

'They seem very plentiful. One stung me in the ear just now. And now one of them has knocked off my hat. Most extraordinary.'

A man in a walrus moustache who had played for Surrey in 1911 came along, and Lord Plumpton greeted him cordially.

'Hullo, Freddie.'

'Hullo.'

'Good game.'

'Very. Exciting.'

'Wasps are a nuisance, though.'

'Wasps?'

'Wasps.'

'What wasps?'

'I don't know their names. The wasps around here.'

'No wasps around here.'

'Yes.'

'Not in the pavilion at Lord's. You can't get in unless you're a member.'

'Well, one has just knocked off my hat. And look, there goes Jimmy's hat.'

The walrus shook his head. He stooped and picked up a piece of tin foil.

'Someone's shooting this stuff at you. Used to do it myself a long time ago. Ah yes,' he said, peering about him, 'I see where the stuff's coming from. That girl over there in the three shilling seats with your nephew. If you look closely, you'll see she's drawing a bead on you now.'

Lord Plumpton looked, started and stiffened.

'That girl again! Is one to be beset by her through all eternity? Send for the attendants! Rouse the attendants and give them their divisional orders. Instruct the attendants to arrest her immediately and bring her to the committee room.'

And so it came about that just as Conky was adjusting the elastic to his lips a short while later and preparing to loose off, a heavy hand fell on his shoulder, and there was a stern-faced man in the uniform of a Marylebone Cricket Club attendant. And simultaneously another heavy hand fell on the girl's shoulder, and there was another stern-faced man in the uniform of another Marylebone Cricket Club attendant.

It was a fair cop.

The committee room of the Marylebone Cricket Club is a sombre and impressive apartment. Photographs of bygone cricketers, many of them with long beards, gaze down from the walls — accusingly, or so it seems to the man whose conscience is not as clear as it might be. Only a man with an exceptionally clear conscience can enter this holy of holies without feeling that he is about to be stripped of his M.C.C. tie and formally ticketed as a social leper.

This is particularly so when, as in the present instance the President himself is seated at his desk. It was at Lord Plumpton's request that he was there now. It had seemed to Lord Plumpton that a case of this magnitude could be dealt with adequately only at the very highest levels.

He mentioned this in his opening speech for the prosecution.

'I demand,' said Lord Plumpton, 'the most exemplary punishment for an outrage unparalleled in the annals of the Marylebone Cricket Club, the dear old club we all love so well, if you know what I mean.' Here he paused as if intending to bare his head, but realising that he had not got his hat on continued, 'I mean to say, taking pot-shots at members with a series of slabs of tin foil, dash it! If that isn't a nice bit of box fruit, what is? Bad enough, if you see what I'm driving at, to take pot-shots at even the *cannaille*, as they call

them in France, who squash in in the free seats, but when
it comes to pot-shotting members in the pavilion, I mean
where are we? Personally I would advocate skinning the girl,
but if you consider that too extreme I am prepared to settle
for twenty years in solitary confinement. A menace to the
community, that's what this girl is. Busting about in her car
and knocking people endways with one hand and flicking
their hats off with the other, if you follow my drift. She
reminds me of . . . who was that woman in the Bible whose
work was always so raw? . . . Delilah? . . . No . . . It's on
the tip of my tongue . . . Ah yes, Jezebel. She's a modern
streamlined Jezebel, dash her insides.'

'Uncle Everard,' said Conky, 'you are speaking of the
woman I love.'

The girl gave a little gasp.

'No, really?' she said.

'Absolutely,' said Conky. 'I had intended to mention it
earlier. I don't know your name . . .'

'Clarissa. Clarissa Binstead.'

'How many s's?'

'Three, if you count the Binstead.'

'Clarissa, I love you. Will you be my wife?'

'Sure,' said the girl. 'I was hoping you'd suggest it. And
what all the fuss is about is more than I can understand.
Why, when we go to a ball game in America, we throw pop
bottles.'

There was a silence.

'Are you an American, madam?' said the President.

'One hundred per cent. Oh, say, can you see . . . No, I
never can remember how it goes after that. I could whistle
it for you.'

The President had drawn Lord Plumpton aside. His face
was grave and anxious.

'My dear Everard,' he said in an urgent undertone, 'we
must proceed carefully here, very carefully. I had no notion
this girl was American. Somebody should have informed
me. The last thing we want is an international incident,

particularly at a moment when we are hoping, if all goes well, to get into America's ribs for a bit of the stuff. I can fully appreciate your wounded feelings . . .'

'And how about my wounded topper?'

'The club will buy you a new hat, and then, my dear fellow, I would strongly urge that we consider the matter closed.'

'You mean not skin her?'

'No.'

'Not slap her into the cooler for twenty years?'

'No. There might be very unfortunate repercussions.'

'Oh, all right,' said Lord Plumpton sullenly. 'Oh, very well. But,' he proceeded on a brighter note, 'there is one thing I can do, and that is disinherit this frightful object here. Hoy!' he said to Conky.

'Hullo?' said Conky.

'You are no longer a nephew of mine.'

'Well, that's a bit of goose,' said Conky.

As he came out of the committee room, he was informed by an attendant that a gentleman wished to speak to him on the telephone. Excusing himself to Clarissa and bidding her wait for him downstairs Conky went to the instrument, listened for a few moments, then reeled away, his eyes bulging and his jaw a-droop. He found Clarissa at the spot agreed upon.

'Hullo, there,' said Conky. 'I say, you remember me asking you to be my wife?'

'Yes.'

'You said you would.'

'Yes.'

'Well, the words that spring to the lips are "*Will* you?" Because I'm afraid the whole thing's off. That was MacSporran on the 'phone. He said he'd made a miscalculation, and my tenner won't be enough to start that sea water scheme going. He said he would need another thirty thousand pounds and could I raise it? I said No, and he said "Too bad, too bad." And I said: "Do I get my tenner back?", and he said: "No, you don't get your tenner back." So there you are. I can't marry you.'

Clarissa wrinkled her forehead.

'I don't see it. Father's got it in gobs. He will provide.'

'Not for me, he won't. I always swore I'd never marry a girl for her money.'

'You aren't marrying me for my money. You're marrying me because we're soulmates.'

'That's true. Still, you appear to have a most ghastly lot of the stuff, and I haven't a bean.'

'Suppose you had a job?'

'Oh, if I had a job.'

'That's all right, then. Father runs a gigantic business and he can always find room for another Vice-President.'

'Vice-President?'

'Yes.'

'But I don't know enough to be a Vice-President.'

'It's practically impossible not to know enough to be a Vice-President. All you would have to do would be to attend conferences and say "Yes" when Father made a suggestion.'

'What, in front of a whole lot of people?'

'Well, at least you could nod.'

'Oh yes, I could nod.'

'Then that's settled. Kiss me.'

Their lips met long and lingeringly. Conky came out of the clinch with sparkling eyes and a heightened colour. He raised a hand to heaven.

'How's that, umpire?' he cried.

'Jolly good show, sir,' said Clarissa.

Herbert Wins the Toss

by BEN TRAVERS

Although that completes my Select XI, the vagaries of authorship being what they are, it would seem to be wise to have a twelfth man along in case of absence or injury. Who better than the venerable Ben Travers, the master of farce, who wrote about his lifelong fascination with the game in a remarkable memoir he called 94 Declared, *which was published a year after his death in 1980!*

Ben began playing and reading about the game as a schoolboy at the Abbey School in Beckenham and later at Charterhouse. He continued to play while making a name for himself as a novelist and dramatist in London, and occasionally during his service with the RAF in both World Wars. Even when fame embraced him after the publication of Rookery Nook *in 1923, he still considered his greatest honour was being elected to membership of M.C.C., and in* Who's Who *he listed 'watching cricket' as his favourite hobby. Like most of the other contributors to this volume, Ben had no time for those who were forever trying to find deeper meanings in the game. 'The one genuine and original reason for cricket,' he said, 'is for FUN!' You will find few better examples of a writer practising what he preaches than in this next story.*

191

IN the early days of summer, when a belated attack of influenza had left me feeling like a bit of partially-chewed string, I had accepted an invitation from Herbert's wife to recuperate in the country.

On the eve of starting, a wire came from Herbert, which read: 'Bring flannel—Important.' I was rather puzzled by this, and, as we sat over our cigars the next night, I questioned him on the matter.

'Why', I asked him, 'did you send me that wire about flannel?'

'Flannels—plural,' he corrected me. 'Cricket flannels! If the wire said flannel, it was a mistake!'

'Cricket flannels!' I repeated. 'What for?'

'Cricket.'

'I'm afraid I don't quite get you,' I said. 'Are you and I going to play tip and run for the sheer joy of the thing, or is it some new health-stunt?'

Herbert's reply seemed irrelevant.

'I was talking to the Vicar the other day,' he said, 'and I must say I entirely agree with him.'

I find much of Herbert's conversation hard to follow even when my mind is clear. Bemused with influenza and vintage port, the task seemed hopeless.

'I've never met a Vicar I entirely agreed with yet!' I said. 'What were you discussing? Theology?'

'No! Cricket!'

The man was getting on my nerves.

'Don't keep on saying cricket!' I implored him. 'Tell me, in a few well-chosen words, what you're getting at!'

He fixed me with a truculent eye.

'It's a positive disgrace,' he said sternly, 'that a village of the size of Great Bosham should have no cricket club.'

I was rather cowed. He seemed to think it was my fault.

'Quite!' I murmured meekly.

'Kipling may talk about flannelled fools,' he went on, warming to his subject, 'but where was the battle of Waterloo won?'

'Let me see!' I said. 'At—er—Waterloo—was it?'

'On the playing-fields of Eton, my boy!' he answered himself. 'There are plenty of fields in Great Bosham, but no players.'

'Shameful!' I said. 'But can't it be remedied?'

'It can. And what's more, it's going to be. That's where *we* come in.'

'Is it?' I said. 'If a small donation would help, of course, I'd be very glad to—'

'No! No! What's needed is active support.'

I coughed nervously.

'You're not seriously suggesting that you and I should set the cricket-ball rolling, so to speak, are you?' I asked.

'The Vicar is arranging a trial game on Saturday, and I have promised to play.'

I looked at him in dismay. His is not an athletic figure—besides, I have seen him on the golf-links.

'I'd no idea you were a cricketer,' I said.

'Well, I haven't kept it up, but I should probably have had

my third-eleven colours at school if I hadn't had chicken-pox.'

'Ah, well!' I said. 'One can't have everything.'

'I told the Vicar I should have a friend staying with me, and he said he hoped you'd turn out too.'

This seemed the moment for firmness.

'I hate to disappoint the Vicar,' I said, 'but I haven't played cricket for thirty years, and even then, I was only in the "rabbit" class. Besides, I'm a sick man, remember!'

'Well, then, you must umpire or score.'

It struck me that if Herbert were a fair specimen of the batting-strength, the job of scorer should be a soft one.

'Certainly,' I said. 'I'll keep the score for you, if I shouldn't catch cold sitting in the pavilion.'

'There isn't any pavilion to sit in. There's a sort of a shed for the players to change their trousers in—those that have got any.'

I looked shocked.

'Surely', I said, 'the Vicar wouldn't countenance anyone playing without them.'

He frowned at me.

'Don't be absurd!' he snapped. 'I meant flannel trousers.'

His mind seemed full of flannel.

Herbert is apt to ride his hobbies hard, and I soon saw that this cricket tomfoolery was to be no exception. Next day he motored to the neighbouring town, and came back laden with bats, pads, balls and other paraphernalia—also, a book on cricket, by the world-famous Jack Blobbs. In the evening, he read a chapter entitled 'Hints to Young Players' aloud to his wife and me, in an endeavour, I supposed, to recapture his lost youth.

After this, life in the immediate vicinity of Herbert became dangerous. I would come upon him in the dark places of the hall and passages, swinging cricket-bats, walking-sticks or umbrellas wildly in the air, practising forward-drives, late-cuts and leg-glances.

'Jack Blobbs says', he explained to me, having missed my

face by inches, 'it's a matter of wrist, foot-work and timing the ball, but what you want most is a good eye.'

'I shall certainly be wanting an eye presently,' I agreed tartly. 'You nearly put mine out just now. Couldn't you shout "Fore!" or something, when you feel these paroxysms coming on?'

But he was deaf to my protest.

'Follow the stroke right through,' he burbled on, 'keeping your—confound!'

The bat he was flourishing had made a nasty mess of the hall mirror.

'That's seven years' bad luck!' I said cheerfully. 'I'm afraid you won't make a century now.'

His ardour was only momentarily damped, however.

'I'm having an hour's net-practice this afternoon,' he told me. 'The gardener's putting up a net on the lawn now.'

'You're not expecting me to bowl at you, are you?' I inquired.

'No! no! I want some *real* practice. The Vicar's got a young nephew staying with him—can't go back to school because of some epidemic—he's coming—and old Colonel Crowfoot's new chauffeur, Sparks. He's reported to be a demon bowler—very fast.'

I began to feel sorry for Herbert.

'Be careful!' I said. 'Stand well away from the wicket, in case either of them can bowl straight!'

Herbert bridled.

'You seem to forget', he replied with dignity, 'that I'm not quite a novice at the game.'

Evidently, he was determined to do or die, so I left him to his fate. Strolling out on to the lawn after lunch, I found him buckling on his pads. Somehow his make-up didn't seem quite right. He was arrayed in a very large sweater, grey flannel trousers, brown canvas shoes, and a tweed cap. Nearby stood the youth from the Vicarage, in immaculate 'whites', and the demon Sparks, in shirt-sleeves and a sheepish grin.

Herbert took his stand at the wicket, and the Vicar's nephew sent down a slowish half-volley. It was a ball that deserved to be hit into the next county; but it chanced to be straight—so Herbert's stumps were spreadeagled.

'Were you ready, sir?' inquired the youth tactfully. He is a nice-mannered boy.

'Not quite!' lied Herbert.

While he was demonstrating to me how Jack Blobbs would have played the stroke, Mr Sparks, in a fit of demoniacal frenzy, took a run of several yards, and hurled the ball, full-toss, at him, hitting him on the groin. He dropped to the ground, and lay there, groaning in anguish. The Vicar's nephew and I did what we could in the way of first aid, and after a course of abdominal massage, I led a limp and chastened Herbert back into the house. This put the lid on any further net-practice, but he continued to study the theory of the game, as expounded by Blobbs, and to deliver homilies on it to his bewildered wife and me.

One way and another, I was thankful when the great day arrived. The two trial teams might have been fairly described as Improbables v. Impossibles. Herbert was to figure among the Impossibles, officially labelled 'The Vicar's XI'.

The Vicar, in his wisdom, contrived to get called away to a convocation in a neighbouring town at the eleventh hour, and sent an S.O.S. to Herbert asking him to deputise as captain.

I believe I was more rattled than Herbert over this ecclesiastical default. Fools, I reflected, step in where vicars fear to tread.

We set out for the ground in the car immediately after lunch. Of the many fields in Great Bosham, the embryo cricketers seemed to have pitched on the worst. A small patch of grass in the middle of it had been cut, but the outfield resembled a jungle more than a cricket ground. The wicket was more of a 'bumper' than the attendance, although Herbert's wife and one or two other local celebrities were expected later. A representative gathering of cows, and one bull, of a singularly forbidding aspect, peeped over Farmer Stiles' adjoining hedge in resentful wonder.

The Improbables, who included the demon Sparks, were skippered by Ben Honeybun, the landlord of the 'Giddy Goat'—a man built on generous lines, fore and aft.

Herbert won the toss and put the scratchiest-looking 'scratch eleven' I have ever seen in to bat. Their one ray of hope was the Vicar's nephew.

Two of Great Bosham's oldest inhabitants had been lured from the bar-parlour of the 'Giddy Goat' to act as umpires. One was 'hard of hearing, and, so, deaf to all "appeals" '. The other, anxious to get through with the business and return to his quart-pot, shouted 'H'out!' whenever called upon for a decision. In this way, the batsmen's chances were, at least, more level than the pitch.

I seated myself on a bench, sharpened a pencil, and prepared to record the score, if any.

The first two batsmen lacked enterprise, but, since the opening bowlers also lacked the ability to bowl straight, they managed to keep their ends up for some minutes. Then one of them, despairing of ever hitting the ball, hit his wicket instead.

Events speeded up when Sparks was put on to bowl. True, he hit the stumps less frequently than the batsmen, but the results were equally effective. He caused two faint hearts to 'retire hurt' in his first over, and the rest of the innings consisted in the efforts of terror-stricken men to escape with their lives, by getting themselves out as quickly as possible.

My concern for Herbert's safety had made me suggest to him that it would be etiquette, as captain, to put himself in last, and his wife, fearing premature widowhood, had backed me up.

When he went out to bat the score stood at twenty-six for nine wickets, to which the Vicar's nephew (shaken, but still standing up), had contributed twenty 'not out'. Sparks' first ball to Herbert hit him on the knee. The second, a short-pitched one, 'got up' and caught him on the point of the jaw. Then he fell down, and allowed the third to sail harmlessly over his prostrate form to the boundary. By this time his wife, seated beside me, was on the verge of a nervous breakdown; but, fortunately, 'Over' was called, and the strain was relaxed.

The Vicar's nephew cut the next ball sharply to 'point', where Mr Honeybun was standing. It hit him in the midriff, and doubled him up, the ball being lodged securely in the creases of his abdomen. Whether it remained there long enough, before he unbent and let it fall to the ground, to warrant a catch being allowed is a question for the ruling of the M.C.C. At all events, the thirsty umpire, mindful that the 'Giddy Goat' re-opened its doors at 5.30, shouted 'H'out!' and Herbert was restored, more or less intact, to his anxious spouse.

'I'm sorry,' he said to me, during the tea-interval, 'that I didn't break my duck.'

'Don't be sorry!' I replied. 'Be thankful! You might have broken your leg, or, worse still, your wife's heart.'

'Sparks *is* rather a dangerous bowler,' Herbert agreed.

'He isn't a bowler,' I said, 'he's a homicidal maniac.'

'Talking of bowling,' said Herbert, 'I'm in rather a fix. There's only one on my side, the Vicar's nephew, and I can't put him on at both ends, can I?'

'It's not usual. But why not try yourself?'

His eyes lit up.

'D'you think I'd better, really?'

'Certainly!' I assured him. It might at least, I thought, supply a touch of comic relief.

He set his teeth.

'I will,' he said, with a fervour worthy of a bridegroom.

Herbert's bowling was sensational, if nothing else. I should describe him as a fast, slow-medium, off-theory bowler, with a leg-swerve. Starting his run near Farmer Stiles' hedge, he re-emerged suddenly from behind a tree, and sent down a deceptive odd-length ball, which pitched near cover-point, and went away sharply in the direction of the village. Still, he managed to keep the batsmen, the wicket-keeper, the umpires and the spectators all guessing.

The demon Sparks, who proved to be a hurricane hitter, was getting his eye in, and had already hit two sixes and one cow, when things took a dramatic turn. Suddenly, by some freak of fortune, Herbert delivered a perfectly straight ball. As it left his hand, he saw a look of glazed horror come over the Demon's face. To his surprise, Sparks made no effort to play the ball (which hit his middle stump), but threw down his bat and bolted towards the dressing-shed, followed, in close formation, by the rest of the players, with the aged umpires hobbling in their wake.

For a dazed moment, Herbert thought that the shock of his unexpected bowling-feat had unhinged their minds. Then he was conscious of strange sounds behind him—a muffled roar, and the thud of galloping hoofs. Turning round, he saw Farmer Stiles' bull coming, hell for leather, straight at him.

Anxious, doubtless, to avenge his lady friend, the cow, on whom one of Sparks' hefty hits had descended, the vicious brute was further exasperated by a red-silk scarf which Herbert wore round his middle.

Losing his head, Herbert took to his heels and fled towards the farthest hedge, that of the Vicarage garden.

It was a fine race, watched with breathless interest by the spectators who, at a safe distance, rejoiced that, at last, they were to be treated to a sporting event worth looking at.

Herbert had a few lengths' start, but the bull's superior condition told, and, in a ding-dong finish, he caught his man, literally, on the post—the Vicar's garden gate post—and tossed him neatly over the hedge, into a cucumber-frame.

The Vicar's gardener, weeding peacefully, was rather taken aback by having Herbert suddenly thrown at him, as it were. The Vicar's nephew and I had hurried to Herbert's aid, and disentangling him from the débris of cucumber and glass, bore him off to his car, bruised and battered, but gloriously happy at having bowled a man out for the first (and, no doubt, the last) time in his sporting career.

After dinner that night the Vicar rang up to ask how the match had gone off.

Herbert had been put to bed by his wife, so I answered the 'phone.

'Splendidly!' I replied.

'Capital! Capital!' chanted the Vicar. 'And which side was victorious?'

'It was a draw in the bull's favour. Herbert made an admirable captain—he won the toss—twice.'

I'm afraid the Vicar thought I had been dining not wisely, but too well.

Anyhow, he rang off without even saying 'good night.'

The Pitch We Come To

by RUDYARD KIPLING

Any game of cricket—be it a Test Match or a friendly fixture on the village green—will attract its commentators: either the great men of words like Neville Cardus and John Arlott, or the local worthy who 'once played a bit himself' and will readily and without invitation explain precisely what is wrong with the modern game and its players. All these commentators express a wide range of opinions, and the remaining six stories in this collection are by writers with varying degrees of interest in the game and each, of course, inspired by humour.

Rudyard Kipling was one of those with a rather low regard for cricket, and he it was who coined the famous term 'flannelled fools'. While he was living in India around the turn of the century, however, he did watch the occasional game, usually as part of his duties as a journalist on the Civil and Military Gazette in Lahore. *He could hardly fail to become aware of the enormous public interest in the game—and the amount of space the newspapers, his own included, gave to reporting matches. In October 1890, he wrote the following item making fun of the papers for devoting more column inches to cricket than to 'real' news. This amusing parody has never been republished in Kipling's collected works, so I am delighted to be returning it to print here for the first time in a hundred years.*

SCENE: *Begum Nugger, B-mbay Presidency.*
Newly arrived Competition-wallah and Oldest Inhabitant.

N.A.C.W. (Opening *Times of Hindustan*) *loq.* to *O.I.* — 'I suppose that one can obtain all the daily news of the Empire in this the apparently leading newspaper of this Presidency? No need to take one in from Bengal or Madras in order to keep *au courant* with affairs?'

O.I. — 'Oh, ah yes . . . Certainly. Never read more than the telegrams myself, but you'll be sure to find all you want in the *Times of Hindustan*. Want to buy a horse?'

N.A.C.W. — 'Thanks not yet.' Determines to take in *Times of Hindustan* for a month. Does so. Reads it steadily and finds the telegrams, &c., run as follows (with a few slight variations in Reuter's from Europe) from the 1st to the 30th:

LATEST TELEGRAMS

RIOTING IN IRELAND
Mr O'Blather has been arrested.

ANOTHER MILITARY MUTINY
Drummer Atkins has broken his drumhead in a fit of insubordination.

WAR IMMINENT
All the European powers are arming.

CRICKET

P_____&c.

The cricket match between the Veterans and the Griffs, which we all know is of the utmost importance and on which one may say so many political issues hinge in this Presidency, commenced today in a burst of sunshine—real Governor's weather—on a wicket of perfection, smooth as an English graveyard and hard as a macadamised road. The sides were generally considered to be so evenly matched that, allowing for the usual intervals for refreshments, the match, if properly played out, will last a week. Public business will of course be suspended during this period to admit of H.E. the Governor and his *entourage* being constantly present, as well as to enable the Members of Council, Secretaries to Government and other leading personages of the Presidency to attend daily. The greatest interest is evinced in the game by the large numbers of spectators and the Parsees have sent their Chamber of Commerce to witness the event. Mr Vobis and Dr Nobis acted as umpires with a true British spirit of justice, partiality and effection, while the Hon'ble Mr Muzfuz, having 'got wind of the sport', as usual closed his court in order to undertake the onerous duties of scorer, the intricacies of which he has so nobly grasped by long and varied experience in the Presidency. Indeed, he has disinterestedly deferred judgment in the trifling cases before him in consequence—public-spirited action which is much admired in the Presidency.

Play commenced punctually one hour after the time stated to give the Veterans an opportunity of digesting their last night's supper at the _____ club and their *chota-hazris* of whiskey and soda (the former supplied by Messrs T-ch-r and Co. at Rs.38 the dozen). The Griffs won the toss and sent in Messrs Snooks and Flooks to the bowling of Major Florid and Mr Torid. The first wicket fell for 0 amidst a round of applause from the spectators, in which His Excellency the Governor joined heartily. Play was then adjourned to hear the opinion of His Excellency the Governor upon a 'duck's egg', and the manner in which he would lay down the cricketing law upon the way this was laid. 'A duck's egg' said H.E. the Governor, 'is laid upon an average. But in my opinion the laws of cricket on this point need reform, as an average of duck's eggs leads to nothing. But, gentlemen and cricketers, remember that in my position here, when anything I may state may be used in evidence against me— ahem, I mean may be turned to political purposes—I must leave it to you, gentlemen, to study the laws of cricket yourselves, and when in doubt give the egg the benefit of it—do not addle it, so to speak.' (His Excellency's remarks were greeted with continuous applause, in which the Parsee Chamber of Commerce fully joined.) Precisely at five minutes before 2 p.m. the game proceeded, when Lieutenant Flooks was succeeded by Mr Trundle. Trundle hit freely, but before he could increase the score was taken cleverly at the wicket, after hitting it, by Dr Muffler, who would have kept wicket splendidly had not the bowling been swift and inclined to leg. In order to equalise this Mr Poker was put on to bowl while Lieutenant Stoker went in. He had added a brilliant cut of one to the off, when the tiffin bell rang, much to the relief of the field, who were growing exhausted.

During tiffin several speeches were made and H. E. the

Governor gave his opinion on cricket lunches in general. He said: 'Gentlemen and cricketers, gooseberries and cream and long scores go not together. Let me remind you of this: in fact they play old gooseberry with your play. (Applause to a choking pitch.) You may correct the gooseberries, it is true, with green chartreuse (applause, especially from the Veterans), but nothing green will correct your cricket except the village green; and if you draw your corks too freely you may as well draw your stumps for ever. I may mention that this is mere metaphor without any political significance.' (Great applause.) After tiffin Mr Sniggler went to the wicket to face the bowling of Major-General Von Flareup. Before many overs he made a brilliant cut to square-leg which was stopped by the umpire, who declined to stay out any longer in such a position.

Fortunately, Mr Jerkeminjeebhoy, who was a spectator, offered to replace him, but unfortunately this led to a some-what disagreeable dispute, which, however, was settled on appeal to H.E. the Governor, who stated that: 'The umpire's decision should be final, but as, gentlemen, this in a great measure depends upon the weather and the laws of cricket need often some interpretation, I would recommend you to refer the question to the M.C.C., as otherwise, in my posi-tion here, such a ruling might be construed to contain some class or political inference.' Major-General Von Flareup then withdrew his objections and play proceeded, and the next three wickets fell for six runs. Here another slight *contretemps* occurred as Mr Thugden O'Tule made some hint about a P – – na 'rot' having set in; but no offence being, it appears, meant, the game continued and H.E. the Governor did not leave the ground as was at first feared. Then Stoppinger went in. He had come all the way from Kirkee to play, and this high-spirited action was much and deservedly applauded, especially as he had arrived in time to bat. He is the *pièce de résistance* of the Griffs' team and comes with the reputation of being a beautiful bat and superb bowler. Indeed H.E. the Governor remarked that he could see with half an eye that he was a born cricketer from the way in which he buttoned his gloves and stopped play for over five minutes as a large butterfly was hovering over the bowler's arm. He was clean bowled the first ball amidst thunders of applause. He met with much sympathy, especially as he candidly admitted the ball was a straight one. Stoppinger was followed by Fiddlekins . . .

C.W.—'Oh hang it all! Can't read through all this; let's see who won' (looks at end of telegram). 'This closed the innings for the Griffs, Fiddlekins, who defended his wicket carefully in spite of a sore nose, having carried his bat for four . . .' (with a sigh)—'I suppose some one at the Club will tell me who has won.' Now for the other telegrams. Reads—

CRICKET

Y.M.C.A. vs. Hindus.—This match was commenced at ____ on the ____ and a general holiday was preserved in consequence. The Y.M.C.A. eleven . . . &c. (here follow particulars).

Reads next telegram.

CRICKET, B____B—Y

'A large and influential gathering took place today to discuss the question of Mr Jerkeminjeebhoy's bowling, and it was unanimously determined to send a deputation to ask H.E. the Governor to give his decision in the matter.'

Goes on to the next telegram.

CRICKET AT MUGGUR

'This place has been *en fête* for the last week on account of the annual match of the Parsees v. The Station. A dispute having arisen during the match regarding the exact position of Mr Legbeforewicketwallah's big toe it was determined to refer the matter to H.E. the Governor for his decision, &c.'

Reads next.

BALL AT P_____

'A grand ball was given by the members of the – – – – Club at their premises last night. The grounds were beautifully laid out as cricket pitches, the stumps lending a realism to the scene, while the rooms were tastefully decorated with cricket bats and balls. Great credit is due to Messrs – – – – and – – – – – for the originality of the idea, and His Excellency the Governor and Lady – – – – expressed their high appreciation. His Excellency the Commander-in-Chief was also present and appeared to be pleased with the kala-juggers decorated with polo-sticks and balls, and which he insinuated were more fatal than the game as about to be played under the recent G.O. Dancing was kept up till the small hours.'

C.W. – 'Ah! here is something more intellectual.' Reads –

THE D – – – – COLLEGE

'H.E. the Governor, accompanied by Captain – – – – A.-D.-C., visited the College this evening. He made a trite speech on manly sports and told the boys that if they wished to make a forward drive in life they should always play with a straight bat. This has given an impetus to cricket.'

N.A.C.W. – 'Oh! here's some news at last. I've heard of B – – – – y, that centre of – Eh – what? Cricket again!!'

B – – – – y, &c.

'The Ladies' team has been practising for the last week under the able direction of Mrs – – –. We hear that her chief difficulty lies in trying to persuade her fair eleven to discard high-heeled boots and rings and adopt a rational cricket costume instead, and it is proposed to send a deputation to H.E. Lady H – – – for her opinion in the matter.'

C.W. after two columns of cricketing telegrams turns to the letter-press and finds – short leader on Finance, and then long leader on – cricket again! A question of dispute between B – – bay Gymkhana and Parsees. Reads paragraphs and extracts from up-country papers on current topics, and then reads the letters to the Editor.

No. 1.—To the Editor, *Times of Hindustan.*

Sir,—In the recent cricket match between, &c., &c.

Bumbleputtywallah,

Capt. Embryo Hindu C.C.

Groaning in spirit he goes on to the next.

To The Editor

Sir,—It may be of interest to your readers to know that in a cricket match played between Kent and Surrey during the reign of the late Queen Anne one *Myddle-de-Stumpe*—a distinguished ancestor of mine who appears to have been a cricketer of no mean repute at that period—made a 'payre of spectakles' as it was then termed.

Antiquary.

N.B.—I enclose my card which you may show to H.E. the Governor should he ask for it.

C.W.—'Oh! Oh! Ooh! Ah!' Gives a sigh of relief and reads. 'News in advance of the mail'—um. 'Cricket averages for . . .!' Tableau!

Tears up paper and takes in the Trombay Gazette instead, only to find that for one column of cricket in the *Times of Hindustan*—he gets two in the Gazette. Driven to desperation he goes to see the Oldest Inhabitant again.

C.W.—'I say, Oldest Inhabitant, are there no other papers in India, or is the whole Press devoted to the cricket interest?'

O.I.—'Eh, Oh! Ah yes! I believe there are one or two other newspapers. There's one in Bengal and I think another in Madras called the Mail, or something like that. B'lieve they give local news. Myself I only read the telegrams. Yes, a lot of cricket on just now—seems more than usual. By the way, I think you said you wanted to buy a horse? No? Have a peg? No! Well, good morning.'

C.W.—Goes home and reflects. 'There's no help for it apparently. Now I see why the Collector asked me so anxiously if I played and whether I could give him a few hints on the latest cricketing terms, rules about declaring the innings at an end, &c., as he shortly expected a visit from the Governor. What was it he said about my encouraging the game among the puttywallahs and mamlukhdars of the district, the latter especially as they are under a cloud. Let's see . . .' After long reflection takes a gloomy view of his future prospects and applies to be transferred to Burma!

Cricket Through the Looking-Glass

by R. C. ROBERTSON-GLASGOW

No one could possibly accuse Raymond Robertson-Glasgow, or 'Crusoe' as all lovers of cricket know him, of being anything other than an enthusiast for the game. Indeed, enthusiast is probably not a strong enough word for this jovial and energetic talker who, with Neville Cardus, helped raise cricketing reporting from mere journalism to an art form. Yet Raymond was no fanatic, and his appearance—not unlike that of the great comedy actor Alastair Sim—was a mirror of his tremendous good humour. He was naturally attracted to cricketers who were characters and could not stand pompous people anywhere on a cricket ground. Fortunately, many of his reports for The Observer *have been preserved in collections, including Alan Ross's bumper volume,* Crusoe on Cricket, *in which he is aptly described as 'the gentle but high-spirited deflater'.*

Raymond was a cricketer himself, playing regularly at weekends in Oxford and Somerset, where he spent much of his time. He was, by all accounts, no mean bowler, and continued to turn out for the Authors' XI until well into his fifties. Although his job entailed writing about cricket at the highest levels, it was village cricket that fascinated him most—especially what he called its 'jokey comedy'—and some of the most interesting essays in his collections are about this very thing. Raymond loved the art of parody, too, and as 'Cricket Through the Looking-Glass' is not included in Alan Ross's selection, it is ideally suited for these pages.

'IT's getting as dark as it can,' said Tweedledum.
    'And darker,' said Tweedledee.
'Let's go and watch the cricket,' said Alice.
'Nohow,' said Tweedledum.
'Contrariwise,' said Tweedledee.
And so they all went, running hand in hand, with Alice
in the middle. They kept passing a large oak tree on which
was nailed a notice saying, 'THIS WAY TO THE CRICKET.'
    'It's the same tree every time,' Alice thought to herself.
    'I know what you're thinking,' snapped Tweedledum,
'and it's not. At least it wouldn't be if it could be. Contrariwise.'
    'That'll be the cricket,' said Tweedledee. 'I smell buns.'
    'But why should buns mean cricket?' asked Alice.
    'They don't,' said Tweedledee, 'at least not at first. Only
if you go on long enough. You see, buns mean beer, and
beer means members, and buns and beer and members means
cricket. Nohow.'
    They had stopped running now, and were walking under
the shade of a huge stone wall covered with ivy, and Alice

was just going to ask if the field was inside, when there was a frightful crash behind them. Looking round, she saw Humpty-Dumpty sprawling on the ground.

'I hope you aren't cracked anywhere,' cried Alice, running up to him.

'No, I'm not,' answered Humpty-Dumpty, 'not so that it matters. But why,' he went on querulously, adjusting his cravat—'why did the batsman want to hit a two? I don't get in, without paying, to see runs scored like this! It's the worst cricket I've ever seen, and I'm compelled by law to fall off the wall if it ever happens. Most provoking. But help me up again, just as a birthday present. I feel all sixes and fours.'

Alice assisted him up with the utmost difficulty. 'He's so *awfully* round,' she thought; 'there's nothing to catch hold of him by.'

When he had regained his seat, he looked down at Alice with much serenity and said, 'It's all right now, the wicket-keeper has fallen asleep, and they're trying to rouse him with toasting-forks. Goodbye.'

'Goodbye,' said Alice, and ran after the brothers, who had shown no interest at all in the catastrophe. She found them engaged in a heated argument. They both swore that it was going to rain. Tweedledum swore it would rain, because it did whenever it could. At last Tweedledee pulled out a watch and said, 'It's later than yesterday. We shall miss our dinner. Goodbye, Alice. Put up the umbrella, Tweedledum.'

'You aren't really going?' faltered Alice. 'Think what you're missing.'

'I never do think,' rejoined Tweedledee, 'at least, not for long. If you want to see the match, go on as far as you can—'

'Farther than that,' said Tweedledum.

'And then it's the first on the right; at least, it will be by then.'

And off they went, still arguing about the rain: one walking backwards, and the other forwards, which they always did when they were really angry, under the shelter of their huge umbrella, although there wasn't a single cloud in the sky.

'Stupid creatures,' said Alice, with an angry pout. 'However, I suppose I must find my way into the field somehow.'

So she walked on till she came to the end of the wall, where she saw a white wicket-gate. There was a till on each side of it, but nobody there to take any money. So she pushed it open, and found herself in the largest cricket field that ever could be imagined. In the far distance there seemed to be a game in progress.

'Oh dear,' sighed Alice, 'the game will be over before I get there.'

At that moment the White Rabbit hurried past, looking anxiously at his watch. 'Oh, heavens!' he muttered; 'oh, my tail and whiskers! Half an hour gone, two runs scored, and no wickets lost. We are certain to lose, quite certain.'

'If you please, sir—' began Alice.

But he took no notice at all, and trotted on, muttering, 'Certain to lose; oh yes, quite certain.'

Alice was ready to cry with vexation, but, looking up, she saw the White Knight riding towards her. Although he was quite close, he fell off three times before he reached her—once to the right, once to the left, and once just anyhow. However, after some delay, he gathered himself together, adjusted his beehive and mouse-trap, and reined up by Alice.

'Hullo,' he cried. 'Stop! Where are you going?'

'To the cricket,' answered Alice, 'but I fear I shall never get there; it seems so terribly far.'

'That's funny,' said the Knight, 'very funny, as I happen to be going there too. But I spent so long fishing on the way that I am rather late. Do you know that fishing is terribly late?'

'I don't think I quite understand,' said Alice.

'Well, you see, some things are early and some are punctual and some are late. Now daffodils and morning-tea are early, fishing is late, but cricket is punctual, almost punc-

tualer than anything. But I think we ought to be there by
the time the match is lost. I suppose you have got a licence?'

'I'm afraid not,' said Alice. 'I didn't know that it was
necessary.'

'No,' mused the Knight, 'not absolutely necessary, but it
always helps. Well, if you haven't got a licence, you must
say that you are a friend of the Queen. Then you may get
in. Not so long ago there was a match, and nobody knew
that they ought to have a licence. They hadn't been told.'

'What happened?' asked Alice.

'Oh, nobody could get in, as all the doors were locked;
but they behaved very well. They sang a few songs and
went home again. But the Queen came soon afterwards, and
when she found everything was locked, and saw the song-
sheets lying on the ground, she ordered every one's head off
all round; but, being quite alone, there was nobody to be
beheaded but herself. It made her so frumious that she boiled.
Did you see my report on that match?'

'No,' said Alice; 'besides, I thought you said that all the
doors were locked. So you can't have seen anything.'

'Oh, well,' answered the Knight, 'that makes no difference. In fact, I rather think that a report of that kind is far
more accurate. It was a pretty piece of work, and ran something like this. You can sing it to almost any tune, Ancient
and Modern:

"Will you bowl a little faster?" said the Dodo to the Gnurk.
"I waited hours for that one, and it's terribly hard work,
For it makes me feel quite vorpal in an uffish sort of way,
To face a manxome bowler on a mimsy summer day."

So the Gnurk (or Feathered Begum) gave a tulgy sort of sound,
And, taking up the ball, he went galumphing all around,
And quoted lines of Shakespeare which were quite beside the mark,
And said, "I'll bowl a ball or two before it gets too dark."

But when he had galumphed about until his face was blue,
And asked mid-on if Edgware Road was on the Bakerloo,

He burst into a flood of smiles, and said it was a shame
To bowl to any borogrove when Dodo was his name.

The White Knight chanted the last line twice over in his curious, dreamy voice, and then, looking around, said, 'There, that will do. That's quite close enough to the cricket. If we go any closer, we shall be burnt.'

'But cricket doesn't burn,' said Alice.

'Oh yes, it does,' replied the White Knight, nodding slowly.

'Everything burns if you go too close—except, of course, toasted cheese. But I must be going now. I have lots of things to do, and several things not to do, and cricket is one of the latter.'

'Don't go, please don't,' said Alice. 'It's all so strange, and I really had hoped . . .'

'Oh, you'll be all right, I should think,' said the Knight. 'I'll introduce you to the Gryphon. He's sitting over there with the Mock Turtle.'

So they went over to the Gryphon and the Mock Turtle, and the White Knight asked them if they remembered Alice, and the Gryphon just said 'Hcjrrh,' and the Mock Turtle looked away and blushed.

'That's fine,' said the White Knight. 'I knew they would be pleased to see you.' And he rode away, looking so queer and gentle, with the sun streaming on his white hair, murmuring to himself, 'I suppose a Gnurk *is* a Feathered Begum. I don't see what else it could be.'

As the Gryphon and the Mock Turtle still seemed rather preoccupied, Alice looked round her to see what was happening. The field, which had seemed so enormous in the distance, she now found to be quite ridiculously small. She was sitting on the left of the Pavilion, which was made of blue china, with a green turf roof and gables of wedding-cake. In front of it sat the King and Queen of Hearts, and behind them stood the Knave with a tray of red jam tarts. At the end of every over he rushed out on to the field with them, shouting, 'Tea interval! Tea interval! Keep your seats and eat your tarts!' Each time he did this, the Jabberwock, who was senior attendant, tripped him up, and all the tarts were spilled on the grass. Then the Jabberwock helped him up, put the tarts on the tray again, and opened the Pavilion Gate for the Knave to go back, which he did with a joyful alacrity that quite amazed Alice.

The state of the game was like this: The Mad Hatter and the March Hare were batting, the Dormouse was keeping wicket, fast asleep. Father William was bowling, and for each delivery he used a different ball. These six balls lay in a pile just where the sawdust might have been. There was a Lawn Tennis ball, a Royal Tennis ball, a Golf ball, a red India-rubber ball, a Ping-pong ball, and a huge Green Balloon. The ball-boy was Father William's son, who handed his father whichever one was needed. The Mad Hatter was batting with a Croquet Mallet, and the March Hare with a Brassie. The wickets, as far as Alice could see, were three storks each end, all standing on one leg. The fielders were the King's Horses and Men, but most of them had wandered away, except for one white horse which *would* nibble the pitch. The umpires, to Alice's amazement, were Tweedledum and Tweedledee. 'How on earth did they get there?' said Alice aloud; 'they went home just now.'

'No, they didn't,' said the Mock Turtle, turning round for the first time; 'that was yesterday, or even longer ago.'

Tweedledum had a huge placard hanging round his neck with 'OUT' written on it, and Tweedledee a similar placard inscribed 'NOT OUT'; and whenever Father William appealed, which he did every ball, they both pointed to their placard.

'You see,' mumbled the Gryphon in a discontented voice, 'they cancel out, those two placards.'

At that moment Father William shouted 'Over!'

Tweedledum, whose business it really was, just opened and shut his mouth like a fish. Father William's son collected all the balls, and they started from the other end. The Mad

Hatter thumped the Dormouse on the head with his mallet, and Tweedledee carried him off and plopped him down behind the other wicket.

In front of the King in the Pavilion there were six rows of penguins, most of them asleep, watching the match.

'What are the penguins doing?' asked Alice.

'Oh, the penguins are the members,' said the Mock Turtle. 'Some of them have been members for a hundred years, and none less than forty years. They are very wise old birds, and they know exactly what to do during the match.'

'And what's that?' said Alice.

'Oh, just sleep, you know, and then wake up at meals, and then just sleep again.'

At that moment there was a terrible commotion and fluttering in the Pavilion. The Jabberwock was dragging one of the penguins on to his feet, and the member was trying desperately to sit down and go to sleep again.

'What in the wide world is happening?' asked Alice.

'Oh, that?' said the Gryphon, 'that's nothing at all. It's the oldest penguin. He always stands up behind the bowler six times during the day to get a better view; he's done it five times now, but he is bound to do it six. It's the law. And the Jabberwock is trying to make him do it once more to complete the number. Because he knows that if he once lets him go really fast asleep nothing will wake him, not even an earthquake or a meal.'

At last the Jabberwock raised the oldest penguin on to his legs. He stood up for a minute or two, flapped his wings, then relapsed again into a deep slumber; on the left of the Pavilion there was an enormous score-board. It read as follows:

BATSMAN No. 1.	TOTAL.	BATSMAN No. 2.
98	1098	100

BOWLERS. — Father William and Father William.
LAST BATSMAN. — Did not go in.
EXTRAS. — 4s. 6d.

Alice looked at it for some time and wondered how on earth the total could be so large. 'It can't be extras,' she thought, 'because they are quite cheap.' So she asked the Mock Turtle how the scoring was managed.

'Oh, that's easy as Latin verse,' said the Mock Turtle. 'You see, the whole point is not to score runs. But as they haven't got a minus sign on the scoring-board, the whole side starts with a hundred runs each. That makes eleven hundred runs altogether. Now as soon as a batsman gets to the wicket he has to be rather careful. He mustn't score any runs, as the side with eleven hundred runs left at the end wins, and any runs that are scored count backwards. But at the same time he musn't get out, as any one who gets out is beheaded at once. That's the Queen's orders. Of course you can bowl no-balls, but they don't count in the score, but—'

'Are entered up in the bill,' interrupted the Gryphon.

'And as many wides as you like,' went on the Mock Turtle: 'They don't count either, but they are useful as—'

'They make the King laugh,' murmured the Gryphon.

'And the byes,' continued the Mock Turtle, 'are purely a matter of form.'

'But why,' said Alice, 'has Batsman No. 1 scored 98?'

'Oh, that's a great pity,' replied the Mock Turtle. 'A piece of carelessness on the part of the March Hare. He was feeling rather frabjous, and persuaded the Mad Hatter to run two for a snick off the Green Balloon. It will probably lose the match. So stupid. . . .'

Purple Pads v. Gasometer

by BERNARD HOLLOWOOD

Bernard Hollowood has been called the best cricket humorist to have appeared in the pages of Punch, *and this is a view that many share. All his writings have been distinguished by a profound knowledge of the game and a wonderful sense of humour. Bernard's knowledge is explained by the fact that he played County cricket for Staffordshire, league cricket for Burslem and latterly club and village cricket. The sense of humour was undoubtedly aided by many insights into the funny side of the game, which he introduced into scores of essays for* Punch *before, during and after his period as editor of the magazine from 1957 to 1968.*

Bernard was a great believer that cricket was the one game that should be played world-wide, and a number of his funniest essays are about the introduction of the sport into unlikely places. My favourite appeared in Punch *in April 1958 and was inspired by a remark by the then Australian Prime Minister, Robert Menzies, that he wished the Americans and Russians had taken up the game. Although the date when Bernard Hollowood envisaged that the two superpowers might just meet on the cricket pitch has passed by, time has done nothing to diminish the humour of his account of the match between Washington Purple Pads and Moscow Gasometer.*

'CRICKET is so splendid a game, so subtle, that when I contemplate the international situation it occurs to me that if only we had persuaded the Americans and the Russians to play cricket, and actually get stuck into it . . .' I needn't go on with Mr Menzies' fine words: they are heard regularly, annually, at smoking concerts and cricket dinners throughout the Commonwealth, in all lands—Holland, Denmark, Brazil and Portugal included—that have fallen under the spell of the king of games and the sport of princes.

Mr Menzies (supported here of course by his political opponent Dr Evatt) was saying what all cricket-lovers sometimes think, that it would be wonderful if the word Tests had nothing to do with H-bombs and fall-out, if boundaries always meant fours and never frontiers. But would cricket *à la russe* and *à l'américaine* still be cricket? Before me as I write I seem to have the score-card of a match played at Lord's in 1984 in what is called a World Series Test. It is between Washington Purple Pads and Moscow Gasometer, and I see that it lasted thirty-three weeks, was attended by 823 neutral observers, and ended in a draw. This was the decision of a plenary session of United Nations (Poland and Canada abstaining).

The start, scheduled for May 1, was delayed for some weeks through a disagreement about the toss for choice of innings. Neither side would accept the use of the other's coinage for this operation, and naturally enough no uncommitted country was anxious to allow its currency to become involved. In the end the Royal Mint issued a special coin bearing the Hammer and Sickle on one side and the American Eagle on the other, but it was a condition of this manœuvre that the metal used should be drawn equally from the Urals and the Rockies.

Winning the toss the Washington Purple Pads elected to bat. After the swearing-in of umpires (Signor Botinelli of Italy and Herr Grautgrub of Eastern Germany) the game began, and the Americans were quickly in trouble. At one stage they were twenty-three for eight, but a terrific hit for six by Franklin S. Shelmerdine of North Dakota (his amateur status at Yale University was afterwards the subject of lengthy deliberations at the International Court at The Hague) brought all the dismissed batsmen back into the game, and the score was edged towards respectability.

At 108 a boundary dispute held up the innings for a few days—the Russians claiming that a fielder on the tarmac in front of the Tavern had been impeded by hostile pigeons, and the Americans averring that the territory in question constituted a neutral enclave. The Gasometer bowlers, Smith and Robinski, formerly of Harwell, were clever though strangely inaccurate. Their best deliveries, clearly borrowed from the world of chess, were a cunning leg-break based on the movement of the knight, and a ball called a 'slanter' or bishop which came with the arm from the extreme edge of the crease.

Before the Russians batted the screens were surreptitiously painted black by a gang of U.S. sailors from the *New Forrestal*, and on a protest were repainted duck-egg blue by members of the Club Cricket Conference. The Gasometer

tactics were interesting. They batted in depth, often with
three or four men at the receiving end, and while they were
able successfully to protect their stumps they seemed constantly in danger of falling to run-out decisions. They wore
neither pads nor gloves and took innumerable hard blows
without flinching.

Herman Axlegrit, the Americans' star bowler, was repeatedly no-balled by umpire Grautgrub 'for pitching', and at
one time no fewer than five of the fielding side were in the
Long Room Sin Bin or penalty box.

The Russians were all out for 2,473. There were no byes.

Going in a second time the Americans reverted to a
rounded bat and showed immediate improvement. Cohen
hit a nice double century, Schwartz got 1,973 and Nielson
notched a very good looking 387. The side collapsed from
2,924 for four to 3,006 all out, and the Russians, left with
only 706 to get, were justifiably jubilant.

The days were now shortening and play each day was
severely restricted. The British Government delayed the end
of Summer Time and promptly lost two by-elections in rural
constituencies.

The world was showing much interest in the game. When
Gasometer reached 124 without loss Latin America
announced that it was thinking of joining the Communist
bloc. Then with the fall of two quick wickets (131) rioting
was reported from Warsaw and Budapest. The Americans
launched two dozen Sputniks and Russia began a new series
of K-bomb tests in Antarctica.

And now play was held up for nearly two months by
torrential rain, and observers were sent up daily to identify
the aircraft said to be responsible for the cloud-seeding. The
official report of the incident (published many years later)
named Chinese and Formosan air guerrillas.

When play was resumed the Russians progressed slowly
to 384 for three and by December 20 had reached 514 for
six. With Christmas shopping in the air most of London's

department stores, including C. & A. Modes, were declared
out of bounds to both teams.

On December 22 a letter signed by 623 members of the
M.C.C. appeared in *The Times*. It pointed out that Britain
considered her duties as host more than adequately performed, that her patience was exhausted, that the square or
table at Lord's was in a shocking condition and could not
possibly recover properly in time for the Australian tour of
1985, that anything, even nuclear war, was preferable to the
desecration of a great game and a noble cricket ground, and
that the signatories would be grateful if the visitors would
getthehelloutofit.

Humiliated, the Purple Pads and the Gasometer hurried
home, and a few days later the Kremlin and the White House
issued simultaneous statements. They told the world that
Russia and America were in complete agreement: cricket,
they considered, was a silly, stupid, boring game suitable
only for second-class powers.

The Australian tour of 1985, by the way, seems to have
been an unqualified success.

Jack the Giant Commentator

by MILES KINGTON

This next story, as its title may suggest, is a skit on the art of radio cricket commentary. In it, Miles Kington has some gentle fun at the expense of those familiar voices which endeavour to liven up the more boring moments of Test and County matches. Miles, an Irishman by birth, has become one of the best known of today's humorists as a result of his many contributions to Punch, The Times, *and* The Independent. *He is another cricket enthusiast with no time for the pomposities of the game. Indeed, though it is true to say that what follows is written tongue-in-cheek, there are some observations about commentators that may well strike the reader as being very close to the truth!*

Jack was a bit nervous. Actually, Jack was more than a bit nervous. Let's face it, Jack was so nervous that he wished he hadn't had any breakfast. Jack was such a wreck he made the *Titanic* look brand-new. As he turned the corner and saw Lord's cricket ground in front of him, his knuckles tightened on the bag he was carrying until they went white and crackled slightly. Jack was about to commentate for Radio 3 on a Test Match for the first time.

His mother had rung him that morning to wish him luck. Then she had rung back to make sure he had had a proper breakfast. The third time she had rung, which was just to find out if he had married and settled down yet, he could have screamed.

'Mother, I'm going to be all right! I'm just going on the wireless to describe the cricket, that's all.'

'Well, be careful, Jack. Some of those Test commentators sound drunk to me. I don't want you to fall into any bad habits.'

'It's Radio 3, mother. Nobody gets drunk on Radio 3.'

Gosh, Jack felt nervous. As he walked towards the headquarters of cricket, he could even hear ringing in his ears. Then he realised what it was; in a telephone box set back against the wall the phone was ringing. Out of sheer curiosity he went in and answered it.

'And another thing, Jack,' said his mother's voice, 'the forecast says it's going to be cool, so keep your jersey on.'

'Yes, mother,' he said weakly and put the phone down.

The commentary box was much as he imagined it would be. A table overlooking the ground, four or five chairs, a TV set out of the way in the corner, a few boxes, pencils, lots of mikes and wires. There was a man in a bow tie in one of the chairs, reading a paper.

'Hello,' said the man. 'You must be Jack, the new boy. I'm Alex Simpson—I think we're doing the same stint together today. Feeling nervous?'

'Just a touch apprehensive.'

'No need, old boy. We'll have a great time together. Lots of laughs. Keep telling stories, that's the main thing, and the older the better. Round about tea-time we read letters from listeners, but of course we've made all those up ourselves. I should have one or two ready, if I were you.'

'Right.'

'Good. Well, I'm off for a cup of tea.'

Left to himself, Jack sat at the table and pulled a mike towards him. Feeling rather silly, he started to speak into it.

'And Botham walks back again, with that distinctive massive stride. Not much luck this session so far, but the thing about Botham is that you never know when he is going to make the breakthrough that England . . .'

'. . . so desperately need,' said a voice behind him.

Jack whirled round to find a tall, gangly man smiling at him. 'You must be Jack,' he said. 'I'm Alex Simpson. I think we'll be sharing the same stint together today.'

'But . . . but the man with the bow tie said he was Alex!'

The man laughed. 'Old George likes his little joke,' he said. 'You know George Stepney, the old Middlesex wicket-

keeper? We bring him in for lunch-time reminiscences—
makes them all up of course, but then we all do.'

The phone rang. Alex answered it. 'It's for you,' he said,
looking oddly at Jack. 'I think it's your mother. I'm off for
a quick one. See you.'

'Mother!' said Jack. 'I don't know how you got hold of
this number, but *never* ring me on it. Do you understand?'

'I don't know what the hell you're talking about,' said a
man's voice. 'Is that Jack, the new boy?'

'Yes,' said Jack in a small voice.

'It's Alex Simpson here. I think we're doing the first stint
together. Tell them I'll be late, will you? Thanks.'

Jack felt as if he were going mad. He wondered if it could
get any worse.

The first thing Jack noticed was that none of the other
commentators seemed to watch the game. That is, they
never looked out of the window. They kept their eyes fixed
on the TV set in the corner, which had the sound turned
off, and described what they saw there.

'And Botham plays at that—and misses!' said the one he
now knew to be called Harvey, a wrinkled ex-spinner from
up north. 'A very airy-fairy shot. Let's see that one again.'

Jack thought it odd that radio listeners should be invited
to see something again that they had never seen in the first
place, but nobody else seemed to find it strange. In fact, Jack
had been watching the shot through the window and
couldn't make out if Botham had hit it or not.

'That's the very same shot that got him out at Edgbaston
in 1982, wasn't it?' said Harvey. 'He'll really have to graft
harder than that, against bowling as tight as this.'

It sounded authoritative, but Jack had just seen a note
passed to Harvey from Sid, the scorer. Sid had a computer
and five notebooks, which he worried at the whole time.
The note had said: 'Same shot, out, Edgbaston, 1982.'

'McIntyre was very fond of that shot,' said the man in the
bow tie, coming awake suddenly. 'Do you remember him

coming in third wicket down against the Australians at
Leeds, 1948, when everything was against us? He flashed
outside the off stump for five overs, until some wag in
the crowd shouted: "He thinks he's conducting the bloody
Hallé." '

'Old McIntyre,' said George. 'What a character he was. I
remember him appealing against Bradman for lbw in 1952,
getting the appeal turned down and handing the umpire a
pair of spectacles!'

During this exchange, Jack noticed, three balls had been
bowled, none of them mentioned by the commentators.
It was at this point that he begun to understand that the
commentary was more important than the cricket, and that
most of what was said had nothing to do with this game at
all. When he came to do his stint, he too found himself
watching the TV and describing it. He even found himself
referring to McIntyre, a cricketer of whom he had never
heard. He was relieved when lunch came.

'One of the unusual features of this game,' said the man
with the bow tie suddenly to the microphone, 'is how
pimply the Australian off-spinner is. How many great spin-
ners with acne can you think of, Jack?'

Jack found himself stammering that there seemed to be no
great correlation between spots and spinning, although Lance
Gibbs may well have suffered from this but it was difficult
to tell, him being black. During the break in the tea-room,
he asked the bow tie man why he had asked such a tasteless
question.

'Well, we weren't on the air,' said bow tie affably. 'I
thought you knew that.'

'What about McIntyre?' said Jack. 'I've never heard of
him.'

'McIntyre is our fictitious cricketer of the day,' explained
bow tie. 'Every day we make up a new historical cricketer.
We also have a competition to see who can keep the same
story going the longest, and another competition to use
words that Harvey can't understand. Harvey's very Lanca-

shire, you understand, and we're trying to knock it out of him.'

During the afternoon rain stopped play for a while and the commentators really came into their own, telling jokes, spinning memories, doing conjuring tricks and reciting poetry. Harvey even sang a couple of songs. Much to his surprise, Jack found himself doing his mouth organ imitation party trick; he never dreamt he would do it on Radio 3.

'We like rain and bad light best,' bow tie told him at teatime. 'There's no cricket to get in the way of the commentary then. Oh, and I never told you. We also sometimes try the odd trick on new commentators. Better watch out.'

Sure enough, half an hour later Jack was describing the field to listeners when he suddenly felt a jug of cold water being poured over his head, slowly and deliberately. It was wet and horrible, but he felt delighted inwardly. It meant he had arrived.

Cricket, Lousy Cricket

by RICHARD GORDON

Richard Gordon may well be more familiar to readers for his famous series of fourteen 'Doctor' novels about the foibles of the medical profession and its practitioners. He turned to novel-writing after a career in medicine, first as an anaesthetist, then as assistant editor of the British Medical Journal *and finally as a ship's surgeon. On dry land, cricket has always been his great love, and he is one of the keenest supporters of Surrey C.C. Occasionally he has been moved to write humorous essays about the state of the game, and 'Cricket, Lousy Cricket' is one such contribution. It was written in December 1966 for* Punch *and was inspired by a questionnaire M.C.C. had sent out to County cricket players in order to get their views about the game. Richard decided to answer the questionnaire from the point of view of a spectator.*

1. Do you enjoy watching county cricket?

Of course not. I go as relief from the widespread obsession, fostered by advertising agencies, that I should be wildly enjoying myself whatever I do. Whether dodging riskily up the M1, appointing the bank my executor, shaving my face, delivering the post, nursing the sick, or joining the Army.

2. Do you believe that present-day county cricket provides good entertainment for spectators?

No, thank heavens. Entertainment has become even less avoidable than enjoyment. Only in unelectronic, untransistorised near-empty county cricket grounds am I confident that no one is going to entertain me in the slightest.

3. If your answer to 2 is 'no,' would you say this is due to lack of incentive to play positive cricket?

They gave the Baltimore Orioles about £5,000 apiece for winning the World Series. On the third day of any county match with the home side playing for a draw this looks cheap at the price.

231

4. Do you believe that the result is more important than the way this result is achieved?

I don't follow. Whoever breathlessly asked the result of *Swan Lake*? Cricket is an art-form, a combination of humanity's two most highly civilised activities, the ballet and the picnic. When I can't get seats for the Test Match I get them for Covent Garden, though the authorities frown on my packets of ham sandwiches and flasks of tea during the interval.

5. Do you believe that the production of hard, fast and true pitches would improve the general standard of play?

Pitches should be as hard as concrete and as uneven as Brighton beach, with regular risk of injury to the batsmen. this will introduce the entertaining blood-sport element of soccer, with television cameras swooping sadistically on players writhing in anguish while everyone else argues fiercely with the umpires. Other lively innovations from soccer would be the return of cricketers' coloured 'strip', and the whole Yorkshire side kissing Fred Trueman whenever he took a wicket.

6. Do you consider that three days is the best duration for a two-innings match?

At least. Cricket is a life-saving activity from Monday to Friday for such layabouts as authors, out-of-work actors, old-age pensioners, redundant car workers, out-of-office politicians, payroll bandits, strikers, and clergymen. And for the wives of all of them.

7. Do you support the idea of limited-over matches as tried in a few matches in 1966?

The more meddling with the rules the better. With every cry of 'No-ball!' I explain perceptively either (a) the crease was cut with the front foot, (b) there had been polishing or other interference with the natural condition of the ball, (c) more than two on-side fielders stood behind the popping crease, or (d) something wickeder occurred than mere straightening of an over-extended arm or use of the wrist in the delivery swing. In fact, the no-ball was released half-way down the pitch, but such authoritative pronouncements do me good.

8. *Many county cricket clubs are at present finding it almost impossible to continue under the present system. How should the county fixtures be reorganised?*

It is not necessary to play any games all summer, though a few cricketers might be retained like the Beefeaters ceremonially to keep alive the memory of past glories. Cricket is strictly speaking a winter activity.

How do we (a) imagine cricket?

White figures shimmering on sun-drenched grass, hours timed by the mellow ticking of ball on willow, snowy marquees crammed with nut-brown ale and hard-boiled eggs, centuries and hat-tricks obtained with speed, grace, and impeccable manners before our half-closed lids.

How do we (b) find cricket?

Sitting on a hard wooden bench in a freezing rainstorm looking at some lengths of corrugated plastic in the middle of a muddy field, glad enough to queue for a sevenpenny teacup of hot water.

It is only contemplation of illusion (a) during the long months of short days filled with such blunt realities of life as frozen pipes and frozen incomes, bronchitis, flat batteries, and politicians on the television, that keeps our national sanity.

Conclusion:

County cricket must be subsidised as part of the National Health.

Bowled Over

by BARRY NORMAN

Barry Norman, the popular presenter of BBC Television's weekly review of the film business, is also one of the most enthusiastic and visible supporters of village cricket. The son of a film maker, Leslie Norman, Barry is an author and journalist as well as a broadcaster, and has played cricket with relish ever since his schooldays at Highgate. He is the author of Sticky Wicket *(1984) and in* Who's Who *lists his favourite recreation as 'playing village cricket'.*

As I began this anthology with Harry Graham's observations on the village game, Barry's contribution on the same topic provides a fitting finale. Although the two authors wrote their stories half a century apart, the words of both underline how little has really changed. And this is surely the reason why Select XIs—such as mine—turn out every summer weekend, and will doubtless long continue to do so.

LETTER from me to Derek Ufton, cricket captain of the Lord's Taverners, in response to an invitation to play in a charity match at Peterborough: 'Are you *sure* you want me for the eight-a-side game? I'm slow in the field, have hardly any arm, bat solely from memory and get tonked mercilessly when I bowl. Whose side are you on anyway?'

Now you may feel that this assessment of my playing ability errs on the side of modesty. Not so. Every word is true, as my team-mates in the Datchworth Second XI will tell you if asked. Even if not asked they'd probably volunteer it.

It therefore says much for their good nature and for village cricket itself that they still let me play. I suppose it also says something about my own foolhardiness/unquenchable enthusiasm (delete whichever seems inapplicable) that I still *want* to play.

The fact is, I simply can't give it up. It's not just the charm of cricket itself (the most divine way of wasting time ever devised by man) that enchants me; it's the particular appeal

235

of the village game, which epitomises all that is best in this gloriously daft pastime.

In our benighted, class-obsessed country there is no more classless society than a village cricket team. No matter who you are, where you work, which school you attended or the size of your bank balance, all that counts is whether you can play a bit. And if you can't, you can still get by if you try hard.

I've turned out on village greens with or against Earls and Hons and convicted felons, but by that I don't mean the kind of felons with whom Earls and Hons habitually hobnob—bankers, investment brokers and the like—but poachers and gas meter robbers. And for the duration of the match peer and tealeaf would crouch amicably together in the slips with never a thought for the other's pedigree. I've seen professional men and millionaires gaze with awe upon labourers and lorry drivers and wish that—just once—*they* could hit the ball that hard or bowl it that fast.

I first encountered village cricket the year I left school when I, too, could play a bit. (There was a time, I'll have you know, when I opened the batting for Datchworth First XI; never made a hundred but scored several fifties; topped the averages; carried my bat for twelve out of a shameful twenty-six; and once did the hat-trick as an occasional leg-spinner—the 'occasional' part being the captain's idea, not mine.)

Anyway, that summer I played for Ealing Film Studios. I never actually worked for Ealing Studios but my father did and they were short of an opener so I guested for them. One Saturday we took on Sir Michael Balcon's village team and really turned them over—until there strode to the wicket the archetypal village cricketer.

He wore, I promise you, brown trousers and braces, a shirt with no collar and hobnailed boots. Pads, yes, he had those, but he seemed to scorn gloves. I had often read of his like in fiction but I had never seen it before, nor have I since.

Well, naturally, the Ealing dudes in immaculate whites,

multi-coloured caps and club sweaters fell about with mirth. But the yokel was, I imagine, accustomed to this kind of response for he ignored it. He merely ambled to the wicket, adopted a wide-legged stance, implanted his hobnailed boots firmly in the turf and never moved them again. Nor did he need to for he had an eye like a sparrowhawk's.

For the next hour, we of Ealing chased about retrieving the ball from distant parts of Surrey while he scored eighty or so, whereafter—caught on the boundary—he retired to the pavilion, removed his pads, put on his collar and joined us for tea.

At Datchworth, the club I joined some years later after a period of premature retirement brought on by my discovery of women—an admirable species but one which, alas, must carry the blame for curtailing the career of many a fine young player—things were very different.

Whites were *de rigueur* and although the absence of boots was forgiven in the young and impecunious the only officially-sanctioned substitute was tennis shoes. Well, we took our cricket seriously, which is the only way to take it whether you're any good or not.

Discipline was strict, too, but leavened with humanity. The day, for example, when Reg turned up half-cut for an important league match, having come directly from a wedding-reception, his condition evoked the raised eyebrow of surprise and the occasional tut of disapproval but there was no question of dropping him. True, in the field his habit of giggling uncontrollably as the bowler approached the wicket was a touch unnerving, but we solved that by sending him down to fine leg where he could giggle and sing without bothering anyone. We were tolerant, you see. Besides, drunk or sober he was easily our best all-rounder.

In those days I opened the innings with Pete, a carpenter remarkable for never having played forward in his life. This provoked much good-natured derision from those team-mates with pretensions to fancy strokeplay but, since Pete was the first person ever to score a hundred for Datchworth (and the second and third as well), we might have been better emulating him.

I speak now of twenty years ago when the Datchworth wicket, largely unprepared except for cutting and rolling on match days, was notoriously vicious until tea-time. After that it settled down and played as good as gold. Everyone in Hertfordshire knew this except our captain, Phil.

Many a time Pete and I would watch as Phil and the opposing skipper examined the wicket, prodded the pitch, tested the wind and generally gave a passable impersonation of people who knew what the hell they were doing, while we muttered: 'Please God, don't let him win the toss.'

But he always did. He'd come back beaming, one thumb aloft and saying: 'Pad up, lads.' And thirty minutes later Pete and I were back in the pavilion, dismissed by wicked shooters or balls that reared venomously from a good length and Phil would say: 'We've got to find some batsmen.'

Today . . . well Pete's retired and so has Phil, and Reg has moved away. Rex, whose forte is running out his partners, and I are the only survivors of that early team and we're both in the seconds now, under the captaincy of Ron whose ambition is to bowl unchanged from both ends and take a hundred wickets every season, instead of just occasionally.

But so many others have gone, stalwarts like Fat Phil (a different Phil) who used to fart thunderously every time he bent down. For several years he would field—and fart—at silly-point until an opposing batsman complained bitterly of gamesmanship and had him moved. Thereafter his usefulness to the team was greatly diminished and he, too, retired.

I carry on, though, prolonging an inglorious career marked more by scars than trophies—broken nose, broken fingers on each hand, countless bruises on thighs and ribs. But none of these things matters compared with the pleasure and beauty of the game and the wonderful post-match companionship in the bar.

And one thing more: in all the years I've been playing

cricket I've met only two people I didn't like—and I met them both in the same match. My partner and I had put on seventy-odd; I was on forty-seven and he, having been in rather longer, had just touched the ball to leg for two and completed the first fifty of his career. I finished the second run, walked round the wicket and set off to congratulate him. And . . .

'Howzzat!' roared the bowler, grabbing the ball and whipping off the bails.

'Howzzat?' I asked, 'What on earth are you appealing for?'

'Run out,' he said.

'Run out?' I said. 'You must be joking.'

'You'll see if I'm joking,' he said. And turning to that stern, impartial arbiter the umpire, he cried: 'Howzzat, Dad?'

And the umpire raised an index finger and said: 'That's out, son.' And it was.

The injustice rankles still but not too much for cricket, above all games, brings out the philosopher in a man. He who is easily cast down by the slings and arrows will never make much of a player. Mind you, he who is not easily cast down by the slings and arrows may not make much of a player either.

But he is the one with whom I would rather spend my Saturday afternoons on a village green. For he is the one who will appreciate the wicked humour, the irony and the subtlety of the only game that can *always* be guaranteed to bring down the mighty and elevate the lowly. And he will go home a better and wiser man for that knowledge.

Acknowledgements

The editor and publishers are grateful to the following authors, agents and publishers for permission to use copyright stories in this collection: Edward Arnold Ltd for 'Village Cricket' by Harry Graham; Jonathan Cape Ltd for 'How Our Village Tried to Play The Australians'; The Estate of Jack Hobbs for 'The Day of the Duck'; Macmillan & Co Ltd, for 'Five Short Legs' by A. G. Macdonell; Michael Joseph for 'The Unrecorded Test Match' by Lord Dunsany; Methuen & Co for 'The Rabbits' by A. A. Milne and 'Batter Sweet' by A. P. Herbert; Century Hutchinson Publishing Group for 'How's That, Umpire?' by P. G. Wodehouse; A. P. Watt Literary Agency for 'Herbert Wins the Toss' by Ben Travers; The Estate of R. C. Robertson-Glasgow for 'Cricket Through the Looking Glass'; *Punch* magazine for 'Purple Pads v. Gasometer' by Bernard Hollowood and 'Cricket, Lousy Cricket' by Richard Gordon; The Times Publishing Company for 'Jack The Giant Commentator' by Miles Kington; *Expression* magazine for 'Bowled Over' by Barry Norman. While every care has been taken to clear permission for use of the stories in this book, in the case of any accidental infringement, copyright holders are asked to contact the editor care of the publishers.